Unmasking Narcissism:

How to Take Back Your Power in Relationships

Kristin Fuller MS, LCSW

Table of contents

Introduction

If you've ever been in a relationship with someone with narcissism or narcissistic traits, you know how emotionally draining it can be. The games and emotional manipulation played by narcissists are designed to manipulate, control and take advantage of their partners. As a result, victims of narcissist abuse can suffer greatly—sometimes even leading to PTSD, depression, or anxiety. But don't worry; there is good news. Those who have experienced narcissistic abuse can become empowered again and regain their power in relationships with the right strategy. Let's look at how this works.

The first step to reclaiming your power is recognizing the signs of narcissistic traits and behavior. If your partner exhibits any of these red flags, such as a lack of empathy, extreme selfishness, self-centered behavior, or feelings of superiority and entitlement, you could be dealing with a narcissist. Once you recognize that your partner may display narcissistic tendencies, remember that it is not your fault—and that you are not alone!

Once you have identified the behavior as potentially being narcissistic, it is time to begin understanding why it happens —and, more importantly—how to stop it from happening again. For people of narcissist abuse to take back their power in relationships, they must understand the games and manipulation tactics the narcissist play and make a conscious effort not to fall into it again. This means avoiding any situation where they may feel taken advantage of or manipulated by their partner's words or actions.

The next step is learning how to reclaim your life after experiencing narcissistic abuse. Victims of narcissistic abuse need to focus on themselves and build their self-esteem by setting healthy boundaries for themselves and others around them. Additionally, seeking professional help from a therapist or coach can allow victims of narcissistic abuse to gain clarity on their situation and develop coping skills for future relationships. Finally, building supportive relationships with friends and family can give victims an extra boost. At the same time, they work towards rebuilding their lives after enduring emotional manipulation from a narcissist in a relationship.

Taking control over your life after experiencing narcissistic abuse can be difficult, but it isn't impossible! Victims should remember that they are not alone; many people have gone through similar experiences and become stronger than ever! By following the steps outlined in this book – recognizing behaviors in partners who may have NPD (narcissistic personality disorder) or who have narcissistic personality traits, understanding why this happens, and making sure you don't fall into the same cycle again -people who have experienced narcissistic abuse can take back their power in relationships and begin moving forward with confidence once more!

Chapter 1

Sarah's Story

Sarah had been a go-getter all her life. She was naturally ambitious, but it was more than that; she also had an empathetic heart and the desire to help others. When she went off to college, Sarah did not know how manipulative the man she would fall madly in love with would eventually turn out to be.

He was intelligent and handsome, but most of all, he seemed so real - like nothing else mattered when they were together, as if they were soul mates and meant to be. He made Sarah feel as if nothing could stand between them or their love for each other.

Before long, they were married, and as the years passed, Sarah's career had taken off while his had stalled right out of college due to some challenges he faced. Seeing him struggle broke Sarah's heart, so instead of pursuing her dream job, she put everything on hold to support his career and raise their children together - hoping this was what he needed after enduring such hardships early on in life.

However, little did Sarah know at the time that her husband harbored deep dark secrets which revealed themselves gradually over time - covert narcissism being one of them. He became highly controlling and emotionally manipulative towards her and their children - seeming almost disdainful for any success or achievements they may have made outside his radar or approval rating system. It felt suffocating living under these conditions, mainly because it felt as though there was nothing she could do about it since he never openly expressed his dissatisfaction with anything they did wrong according to him, just constant demeaning comments whenever something didn't reach his expectations (which seemed impossible sometimes).

And yet, despite feeling helpless at times, Sarah found strength from within herself, eventually leading up to filing for divorce from him after realizing that no matter what happened during their marriage – good or bad – losing herself along the way is not something she can let happen again ever again. This realization empowered her further until she finally took action by filling out the paperwork necessary for getting a divorce, and her emancipation process began after that!

Overcoming all odds stacked against her newfound freedom, including financial instability caused by having no steady income source, two children who require full attention from her, plus the legal costs associated with divorcing someone hostile – SARAH SURVIVED! As soon as the court accepted the final documents confirming her independence – THAT'S WHEN SHE STARTED TO THRIVE AGAIN! Her ambition returned, albeit slowly but surely, alongside an even bigger fire ignited inside, burning brighter now more than ever before, fueled entirely by self-love & acceptance!! As a result, healthy relationships developed alongside new activities she engaged with helped increase her confidence levels day by day, ultimately making sure this phoenix rose back up strong enough, never forgetting its roots, the same roots responsible for where we are today: standing tall, proud, and facing a future without fear knowing courage lies within every single person who seeks solace through trying times!!!

You Are Not Alone

According to Medscape, it is estimated that NPD is present in 0.5% of the general United States population, and only 2-16% of those who seek help from a mental health professional get the help they need.

When it comes to relationships, narcissists are masters of emotional manipulation. They will try to control your thoughts and desires, making future promises and using emotional blackmail as tools for manipulation. Narcissists may also be more likely to engage in abusive behavior than those without NPD, with Brown estimating that if each person with NPD had an average of 5 partners or close relationships throughout their lifetime, over 60 million people would be affected by narcissistic abuse in the United States alone.

Narcissistic abuse can have long-term consequences on the victim's mental and physical health. Narcissistic abuse victims often experience low self-worth, anxiety, depression, and post-traumatic stress disorder (PTSD). They may also suffer from physical symptoms such as chronic headaches, fatigue, digestive issues, autoimmune diseases, and insomnia. Long-term exposure to narcissistic abuse can lead to a distorted sense of reality, difficulty trusting others, and an inability to make healthy decisions. Victims of narcissistic abuse need to seek professional help to heal from the trauma they have experienced. If you think you may be a victim of narcissistic abuse, it's essential to reach out for help from a mental health professional or domestic violence hotline.

Finding a mental health professional specially trained in trauma recovery and narcissistic abuse can help with healing and recovery. It is also beneficial to partake in self-care activities such as yoga or meditation, which can help heal your mind through your body. Letting go of the need to understand why the narcissist acted the way they did can also be an essential step in the healing process.

Overall, healing from narcissistic abuse prognosis requires patience and dedication. Still, it is possible with the right resources and support system, just as Sarah was able to recover and heal from the many years of narcissistic abuse she endured.

Chapter 2

What is Narcissism?

Narcissism is a term often used to describe someone whose sense of self-importance is inflated and who believes they are superior to others. Narcissistic personality disorder (NPD) is a more severe form of narcissism that can significantly impact people's lives. People with NPD typically show signs of grandiosity, a need for admiration, a lack of empathy, a heightened sense of entitlement, and difficulty in relationships with others. While it's important to note that not everyone with narcissistic traits will develop the full-blown disorder, understanding the signs and symptoms of narcissism can help those affected get the support they need.

Narcissists can also be manipulative and often exploit those around them for their own gain. In relationships, they may exhibit controlling behavior or become overly possessive. Narcissists are also usually quick to anger, act selfishly, or ignore the opinions and needs of others.

Not everyone who exhibits narcissistic traits will have NPD. However, if these behaviors are causing disruption in someone's life—or if it leads to severe distress for themselves or those around them—seeking help from a mental health professional is recommended. Proper treatment and support make it possible to live a healthy, meaningful life.

Covert Versus Overt Narcissism

Narcissism is a set of personality traits and can also become a personality disorder that can manifest in different ways. Overt narcissism is characterized by a blatant display of self-importance and a need for admiration. In contrast, covert narcissism is more subtle and often involves feelings of inadequacy and insecurity.

People with covert narcissism are often introverted and display their narcissistic traits more subtly than those with overt NPD. Covert narcissists have an inflated sense of self-importance and lack empathy for others, but they may not outwardly show this. They may appear humble and self-deprecating, but underneath this false humility lies a need for admiration and validation.

Other signs of covert narcissism include difficulty accepting criticism, a fragile sense of self-worth, an inability to take responsibility for mistakes or wrongdoings, envy or jealousy of others, and manipulation tactics to get what they want. Covert narcissists can be challenging to identify because they don't behave like the stereotypical "narcissist" that we often think of. People who have experienced covert narcissism in personal relationships may have difficulty feeling validated and believed by their family and friends. The covert narcissist will often present a very different picture of themselves in public. In public, the covert narcissist can present as a "nice guy" who is helpful and giving to others. However, behind closed doors, they are a completely different person.

It's essential to recognize the signs of covert narcissism to protect yourself from being taken advantage of by someone with this condition. If you suspect someone may be a covert narcissist, it's important to set boundaries and keep your distance if possible.

Overt narcissists are often characterized by their need for attention and admiration. They may appear generous, sensitive, and loving on the surface. Still, underneath, they are driven by a need for power and control. They are typically the more arrogant type of narcissist who "thinks they are better than everyone else" They often feel entitled to have their way and will lie or manipulate others to get what they want. They can become aggressive or violent if their demands are not met. Overt narcissists also tend to overestimate their emotional intelligence and abilities and display grandiose behavior.

Both types of narcissism can lead to difficulty forming meaningful relationships with others due to their preoccupation with themselves.

Subtypes of Narcissism

Grandiose narcissism is characterized by grandiosity, arrogance, and ambition. People with grandiose narcissism have an inflated sense of self-importance and superiority. They attempt to gain admiration through grand gestures and grandiose behavior. They also have an excessive need for attention, recognition, and validation from people around them. Typical traits of grandiose narcissism include feelings of entitlement, exploitativeness towards others, a lack of empathy or concern for other's feelings, and a tendency to manipulate or take advantage of those around them to get what they want or need. Individuals who possess these characteristics should recognize their unhealthy behaviors before it has damaging consequences on their relationships with others.

Vulnerable narcissism is a term used to describe people with both vulnerable self-esteem and narcissistic traits. Narcissistic individuals tend to display a disregard for the feelings of others, an inflated sense of entitlement (typically from a victim standpoint), and a generally lazy approach toward life. Regarding vulnerable narcissists, however, their negative traits are mixed with qualities that denote vulnerable self-esteem. These vulnerable narcissists can be identified by fear of criticism and rejection, hypersensitivities to positive and negative feedback, low impulse control, and unstable interpersonal relationships. They typically have a "victim mentality" and feel others owe them. In short, vulnerable narcissists exist on a spectrum between what is considered "textbook" narcissism and vulnerable insecurity.

Malignant narcissism is a rarer but incredibly destructive personality disorder. Individuals with malignant narcissism often lack empathy, display aggressive and maladaptive behaviors, and have a sense of superiority over others. They usually operate from an extreme sense of entitlement and continuously manipulate the environment to gain attention and control their surroundings. Characteristics of malignant narcissists include grandiosity, egocentricity, arrogance, harsh judgment towards others, a belief that their feelings and needs are more important than anyone else's, shame projection onto others, guilt-tripping tactics to manipulate people, denial of reality/ exaggeration of facts, lack of accountability for actions or wrongdoings, sadistic tendencies, and trolling or purposely stirring up conflicts to feel superior. They can also be prone to physical violence towards their partners or anyone who triggers their narcissistic rage. People in a relationship with a malignant narcissist should be very cautious and work with a mental health professional to create a safety plan if the narcissist becomes violent.

Superficial narcissism is characterized by superficiality and an imbalance of admiration and entitlement. Those with superficial narcissism often overestimate their capabilities, attention-seeking behaviors, and an inability to empathize or understand the distress of others. This can be evidenced by a superficial preoccupation with physical appearance and superficial charm, empty, shallow one-liners, an obsession with their opinions, and a tendency to calculate social relationships for personal gain. Those with this type of narcissism also have difficulty sustaining relationships, especially those that require mutual respect, trust, and reciprocity.

Neglectful narcissism is a personality trait that involves neglecting responsibilities and feelings and hoarding attention and recognition. Characteristics of neglectful narcissists include ignoring relationships, tasks, and opportunities; having difficulty accepting criticism or blame; being oblivious to the needs or feelings of others; rarely reciprocating, if at all, and trying to manipulate people to benefit their reputation. While narcissistic traits can be present in people with various mental health conditions, neglectful narcissism is particularly damaging because those with it may not realize their behavior is harmful to themselves or others.

Self-righteous narcissism is a set of self-aggrandizing characteristics that blend the self-righteousness of someone convinced they are right with classic narcissism. Not surprisingly, self-righteous narcissists have difficulty empathizing and being aware of their shortcomings. They rarely admit when they make mistakes. Instead, self-righteous narcissists tend to turn the blame for any issue away from themselves and emphasize how "right" their thoughts, words, and actions are. Other trademark traits include a superiority complex and an inflated sense of self-importance or self-worth. It's normal to praise yourself sometimes; however, self-righteous narcissists become defined by their sense of superiority, making it challenging to be humble no matter the situation.

Communal narcissism combines traits of communal behaviors, such as selflessness, kindness, and collaborative thinking, with narcissistic behaviors, such as grandiose behavior. This type of narcissism is often characterized by people who aim to establish strong community relationships but also need to derail others to feel good about themselves. Common traits include over-inflating one's self-importance, turning conversations towards oneself, and attempting to undermine the self-esteem of those around them. While communal narcissists might appear like saints for a cause and are often found in public service arenas, they should be carefully watched since the goal of many communal narcissists is centered on gaining admiration from others rather than building meaningful collaborative relationships. They typically only serve and give to get the recognition they feel they deserve. They can become upset and angered if that recognition is not received.

Cultural narcissists are individuals whose sense of self-worth is mainly derived from their cultural and generational identity. Characteristics of cultural narcissism may include an exaggerated sense of cultural pride, a tendency to prioritize cultural norms over individual needs and preferences, and frequently a rigid interpretation of cultural tradition. Behaviors like performing cultural practices simply because they are expected to or expressing one's cultural identity as superior to other cultures without owing to cultural conflict can be signs someone is struggling with the adverse effects of cultural narcissism. It's important to remember that everyone expresses their identity differently and that problematic traits associated with cultural narcissism can also manifest in a benign or healthy capacity.

What Causes Narcissism

The exact cause of narcissism is unknown, but it is thought to be related to environmental and genetic factors. Childhood experiences, such as excessive praise or criticism from parents, may contribute to the developing of narcissistic traits. Other possible causes include a history of trauma or abuse, significant life changes or transitions, or differences in brain structure or function.

Parental overvaluation has been linked to the development of narcissistic traits in children. Studies have shown that children overvalued by their parents are more likely to develop narcissistic tendencies, such as an overly optimistic self-view and feelings of entitlement. Furthermore, parental overvaluation was the most significant predictor of a child's narcissism over time. Still, interestingly, it did not predict self-esteem.

A recent study published in the Proceedings of the National Academy of Sciences (PNAS) found that parental overvaluation is the most significant predictor of adult narcissism. The research, conducted by a psychology researcher, looked at cross-sectional data to determine what influences narcissism. They found that adult narcissists were likelier than non-narcissists to remember their parents as overvaluing them and lacking warmth. This suggests that parental overvaluation can be a significant factor in developing narcissistic traits in adulthood.

The study also found that other factors, such as aggression, reduced tolerance to distress, and neuroticism may also play a role in developing narcissistic traits. Additionally, research suggests that there may be a genetic predisposition toward narcissism.

Overall, this study provides further evidence for the importance of parental influence on personality development and highlights the need for parents to provide both love and support to their children without overvaluing can lead to feelings of inferiority when the child interacts beyond the family unit.

Child abuse and neglect can have a devastating impact on the development of children, particularly in terms of their emotional and psychological well-being. One such consequence is the development of narcissism.

Research has also found that childhood maltreatment can lead to long-term physical, psychological, and behavioral consequences that may contribute to developing narcissistic traits. Severe neglect has been linked to disruptions in young children's cognitive and executive functions and changes in their stress response systems and brain architectures. Abused or neglected children often show behavioral and emotional difficulties associated with effects on the amygdala, such as internalizing behaviors like depression or anxiety. These experiences can also lead to chronic low self-esteem, poor treatment response, difficulty forming relationships with others, and even fatalities.

Not all abused or neglected children will develop narcissistic traits; however, it is essential to recognize the potential risks associated with parental abuse or neglect so that appropriate interventions can be implemented to support these vulnerable individuals.

How Is Narcissistic Personality Disorder Diagnosed

Narcissistic Personality Disorder (NPD) is a complex mental health condition that can be difficult to diagnose as most people with NPD do not seek treatment or evaluation. It is characterized by an inflated sense of self-importance, lack of empathy for others, and a need for admiration. People with NPD may also have difficulty forming meaningful relationships and struggle with feelings of insecurity or shame.

In order to diagnose NPD, a mental health professional will conduct a thorough assessment which includes taking into account the individual's history, symptoms, and behaviors. The professional may also use psychological tests or questionnaires to help make an accurate diagnosis. Common signs of NPD include having an exaggerated sense of self-importance, feeling entitled to special treatment, and being preoccupied with power, beauty, or success. Other signs include having difficulty forming meaningful relationships and struggling with feelings of insecurity or shame.

According to the Diagnostic and Statistical Manual of Mental Disorders (DSM), NPD includes:

- A pervasive pattern of grandiosity (fantasy or behavior), need for admiration, and with lack of empathy, beginning by early adulthood and present in a variety of contexts.

- A fixation on fantasies of unlimited success, power, brilliance, beauty or ideal love.

- A belief that he or she is special and unique and can only be understood by other special people.

- An excessive need for admiration.

- A sense of entitlement to special treatment.

- Exploitative behavior towards others to achieve personal gain.

- Unwillingness to recognize the feelings and needs of others.

- Envy towards others or a belief that others are envious of him or her.

The DSM criteria also include impairments in personality functioning such as identity disturbance, difficulty with self-direction, and impaired interpersonal relationships. People with NPD may appear dramatic, emotional, or erratic due to their inability to handle criticism or setbacks. They may also have difficulty forming meaningful relationships due to their lack of empathy for others and their preoccupation with themselves. Treatment options for NPD include psychotherapy and medications such as antidepressants or antipsychotics.

It is important to note that not everyone who exhibits narcissistic traits has Narcissistic Personality Disorder. To receive a diagnosis of NPD, the individual must display certain patterns of behavior over time that cause significant distress or impairment in their life. If you think you may have NPD or know someone who does, it is important to seek help from a qualified mental health professional who can provide an accurate diagnosis and create an effective treatment plan.

Is Narcissism Treatable

Treatment for NPD typically involves psychotherapy which helps the person recognize and change their distorted thinking patterns. Medication can also be prescribed to help with symptoms associated with NPD, such as depression or anxiety.

It can be challenging to treat, but evidence-based therapy practices have been found to be effective in treating NPD.

One such practice is Mentalization-Based Therapy (MBT). MBT focuses on helping individuals with NPD understand their thoughts and feelings and those of others. Through this process, they can learn to recognize their own emotions and the emotions of those around them. This can help them develop more meaningful relationships and better manage their behavior.

Another evidence-based practice for treating NPD is Cognitive Behavioral Therapy (CBT). CBT helps individuals identify and challenge negative thought patterns contributing to their narcissistic behaviors. Through CBT, individuals can learn new ways of thinking about themselves and others, leading to healthier relationships and improved self-esteem.

Finally, Dialectical Behavioral Therapy (DBT) is another evidence-based practice for treating NPD. DBT focuses on teaching individuals how to regulate their emotions to manage their behavior better. It also emphasizes the importance of developing healthy relationships with others to foster positive change in one's life.

Overall, several evidence-based therapy practices are effective in treating Narcissistic Personality Disorder. These include Mentalization-Based Therapy, Cognitive Behavioral Therapy, and Dialectical Behavioral Therapy. With the help of these therapies, individuals with NPD can learn how to manage their behavior better and foster healthier relationships with those around them.

It is important to note that treatment for NPD can take time and requires patience and commitment from both the patient and the therapist. With proper treatment, however, individuals with NPD can learn to manage their symptoms and lead more fulfilling lives.

Why Many Narcissists Refuse Treatment

Narcissistic Personality Disorder (NPD) can be a complex condition to understand and cope with, especially for family members and close friends. It is important to remember that narcissists resist getting help because they often lack empathy, have an inflated sense of self-importance, and prefer to blame others. Some may not recognize that their behavior is problematic and thus do not feel the need to seek help. Others may know their issues but feel too ashamed or embarrassed to seek help. Additionally, many narcissists are unwilling to change their behavior because it has become so ingrained that they don't believe it can be changed. However, there are strategies that family members and close friends can use to understand better why a narcissist is resistant to getting help.

First, it is essential to recognize the signs of NPD to understand the narcissist's behavior better. Common signs include grandiosity, need for admiration, lack of empathy, entitlement, and difficulty maintaining relationships. By recognizing these signs in the narcissist's behavior, family members and close friends will understand better why they may resist getting help.

Second, it is important for family members and close friends of a narcissist to practice self-care. This includes setting boundaries with the narcissist so that they do not take advantage of or manipulate their needs. Additionally, those around the narcissist need to take time away from them to maintain their own mental health and well-being.

Finally, it is essential for family members and close friends of a narcissist to seek support from professionals or support groups to learn more about NPD and how best they can support their loved one with this disorder. This will also give them an outlet to discuss any issues or concerns about the situation without fear of judgment or criticism from the narcissist.

If you are dealing with a resistant narcissist, stay calm and avoid engaging in arguments or power struggles. It is vital to set boundaries and communicate your expectations clearly. Do not take things personally; instead, focus on the behavior rather than attacking the person's character. It is also important to practice self-care and maintain your emotional well-being.

It is also helpful to remember that people with NPD can change if they are willing to seek help. Encourage the person to seek professional treatment such as therapy or counseling. Offer support but do not enable their behavior by making excuses or giving in when they become demanding or manipulative. With patience and understanding, it is possible to build healthier relationships even when dealing with a narcissistic personality disorder.

Chapter 3

Cycle of Narcissistic Abuse

N arcissistic abuse is a painful and destructive cycle that can profoundly impact the lives of those who experience it. It is a form of emotional and psychological abuse in which an individual with narcissistic tendencies seeks to control and manipulate those around them. This type of abuse often goes unnoticed, as the narcissistic individual is skilled at presenting a charming and charismatic façade to the outside world.

The cycle of narcissistic abuse can be a complex and challenging experience to understand. It typically involves a repeating pattern of idealization, devaluation, and discard, in which the narcissistic individual alternates between showering their victim with attention and affection and then abruptly withdrawing and becoming emotionally cold and distant.

For the empathetic and sensitive individuals known as empaths, this cycle can be particularly devastating. Empaths are naturally inclined to care for others and are often drawn to those who need help. This can make them vulnerable to narcissistic individuals skilled at playing on their compassionate nature.

It is important to recognize that the cycle of narcissistic abuse is not the victim's fault. It is a deliberate and calculated pattern of behavior designed to control and manipulate those around the narcissistic individual. Understanding the dynamics of this cycle and learning how to identify the warning signs can be an essential step in breaking free from the cycle of abuse and reclaiming one's sense of self-worth and autonomy.

The Idealation Stage

The idealization stage of a narcissistic abuse cycle is the first part of the cycle and one of the most dangerous. During this stage, the narcissist will shower their partner with compliments and attention to gain their trust and admiration. They may be overly generous with gifts and kind words, making them feel like they are truly special and loved. This can include love-bombing, where the abuser showers their target with compliments, gifts, and attention.

Love bombing is a form of manipulation often used by narcissists and sociopaths to "hook" their victims. It attempts to control someone through flattery, compliments, and affection.

Here are 10 signs you may be experiencing narcissistic love bombing in a relationship:

1. They shower you with excessive compliments and attention.

2. They push for an intense connection right away.

They give you expensive gifts or do favors for you without being asked.

4. They tell you what you want to hear, even if it isn't true.

5. They make grandiose promises about the future of your relationship together.

6. They become overly jealous or possessive regarding your time and attention.

7. They try to isolate you from friends and family members who don't support the relationship.

8. They use terms like "soulmate" or "the one" very early in the relationship before they know you well enough to make such declarations of love and commitment.

9. Their behavior is unpredictable - they can go from being intensely loving one minute to cold and distant the next without warning or explanation as part of their manipulative tactics.

10. When confronted about their behavior, they become defensive or deny that anything is wrong at all, making it difficult for them to get out of the situation without feeling guilty or ashamed for speaking up in the first place.

This can be particularly damaging to victims because it makes them develop false feelings of security and dependency on their abuser. It creates an unhealthy power dynamic in which the victim depends on the narcissist for validation and approval, allowing them to become further exploited in subsequent stages.

In some cases, this idealization can also lead to a pattern of intermittent reinforcement where the victim receives positive reinforcement at random intervals. This creates a cycle of psychological torture in which the victim keeps hoping for more validating moments from their abuser, despite being abused repeatedly. This can result in a trauma bond that keeps them connected and makes it difficult to break free.

The Devaluation Stage

The devaluation stage of the narcissistic abuse cycle is when the abuser begins to belittle, disrespect, and degrade their partner to make them feel small and insignificant. This can come in the form of insults, criticism, name-calling, and other forms of emotional or psychological abuse. During this stage, victims become so invested in their relationship with their abuser that they cannot bring themselves to leave or even see their abuser for who they really are.

Recognizing when you are devalued in a narcissistic relationship can be challenging. Here are some signs that may indicate you are being devalued:

- The idealization ends, and you no longer feel special or cherished

- You experience repeated disappointment

- The narcissist puts themselves first, breaking promises and commitments

- They drop subtle hints that you have done something wrong

- They treat you as if you do not exist

- They project their feelings of devaluation onto you

Furthermore, these behaviors may be accompanied by physical isolation from friends, family, or other sources of support and encouragement. This creates an environment where the victim feels utterly dependent on the abuser for validation and approval.

Narcissistic abuse is a form of psychological manipulation and control that can leave lasting effects on its victims. During the devaluation stage of the narcissistic abuse cycle, there are several signs to look out for. These include controlling behavior, gaslighting, censorship, social isolation, lack of boundaries and invasions of privacy, threats and verbal abuse, always walking on eggshells, a sense of mistrust, loss of self-worth, and feeling like you no longer recognize yourself or question your reality.

The Discard Stage

The discard phase, also known as the abandonment phase, is the third stage of a narcissistic abuse cycle. This stage marks when the abuser has grown tired of their partner and no longer needs their services or attention. During this phase, abusers may abruptly end all communication with their victims, either verbally or through text or email, leaving them shocked and empty. Victims may not even be aware that they have been discarded and may cling to hope in vain while waiting for word from their abuser.

Here are 10 signs that a narcissist is discarding you:

1. You're Stronger Than Ever - The narcissist may start to feel threatened by your strength and independence, leading them to discard you.

2. Ghosting - The narcissist may suddenly stop communicating with you without warning or explanation.

3. New Supply - The narcissist may begin to focus their attention on someone else, leaving little time for you in their life.

4. They Change Dramatically - Their behavior may become more erratic and unpredictable as they distance themselves from you.

5. Storytelling - The narcissist may start telling stories about how they don't need or want you anymore as a way of discarding you without actually saying it out loud.

6. Excessive Devaluation - The narcissist may start to belittle and criticize your actions to make themselves feel better about the situation.

Less Emotional Investment - The narcissist may become less emotionally invested in the relationship, leaving little room for connection or intimacy between the two of you.

Other times, discarding can be more subtle. The narcissist will not leave the relationship but act in ways that make it difficult for the other person to stay in it. This can be manifested in ways such as cheating, stonewalling, neglect, etc. Often this is done as another form of manipulation where the narcissist wants to set themselves up as the "victim" when their partner finally feels forced to leave the relationship.

In many cases, the abuser has already moved on to another person who will fulfill their needs in more exciting and novel ways than the former one had. This can lead to feelings of worthlessness, confusion, and betrayal in the victims, who often wonder what they did wrong or how they could have avoided this situation altogether. Victims may experience a range of signs and symptoms that can be difficult to recognize. These include low self-worth, heightened stress levels, depression, anxiety, fear, disorientation, anger, loneliness, and mistrust. Victims may also feel isolated from family and friends and have difficulty setting boundaries or trusting others.

The Hoovering Stage

The final hoovering stage of the narcissistic abuse cycle is a manipulative tactic narcissists use to suck their victims back into an abusive relationship. This stage typically follows the devaluation and discard stages, in which the narcissist has already caused emotional and psychological damage to their victim.

It is a form of manipulation designed to make the victim feel guilty for leaving the relationship and give them false hope that things can be different if they come back. During this stage, the narcissist will often use flattery and compliments to lure their victim back in a while, also making promises of change or improvement to gain control over them again. They may even go so far as to threaten suicide or self-harm if their victim does not return.

One of the most common signs of hoovering is when an abuser suddenly reappears in your life after a period of absence. They may reach out with promises of change or apologize for past wrongdoings, but these are often empty words and should not be taken at face value. Another sign is when they attempt to guilt-trip you into responding to them or giving them what they want. They may also try to make you feel guilty for leaving them in the first place or use flattery and compliments to manipulate you back into the relationship.

Here are some signs that you may be the victim of narcissistic hoovering:

1. Love Bombing - The narcissist will shower you with attention, compliments, and gifts to win your affection.

2. Dramatic Declarations - The narcissist may make grandiose statements about how much they love and care for you or how they have changed for the better.

3. Making Accusations - The narcissist may accuse you of not caring enough or not loving them sufficiently to manipulate your emotions.

4. Threatening to Harm Themselves - The narcissist may threaten to harm themselves if you don't come back or if they don't get what they want from you.

5. Random Calls or Texts Out of the Blue - The narcissist may contact you out of the blue after a period of silence to try and draw you back into their life.

6. Pretending That Your Relationship Isn't Over - The narcissist may act as though nothing has changed between you, even though it has been months since your last contact.

7. Sending Unsolicited Gifts - The narcissist may send gifts or cards in an attempt to win your favor and make up for past wrongs.

8. Indirect Manipulation - The narcissist may manipulate your emotions indirectly, such as guilt-tripping or playing on your sympathies to get what they want from you.

It's vital to recognize hoovering as another form of highly effective manipulation and not engage with the narcissist in any way. It is also important for victims of narcissistic abuse to recognize the signs of hoovering and understand that it is a manipulative tactic designed to keep them trapped in a vicious cycle. Also, remember that no matter how much the narcissist may promise change or improvement, it is doubtful that they will follow through with these promises unless they have gone through intensive counseling and therapy and have genuinely taken self-responsibility for their actions and behaviors. The best way for victims of narcissistic abuse to protect themselves from further harm is by setting firm boundaries and refusing to engage in any kind of contact with their abuser.

If you are stuck in this cycle of abuse, there are ways to find support. First and foremost, it's important to remember that you are not alone and that help is available. Reach out to a trusted friend or family member for emotional support, or consider talking to a therapist who specializes in narcissistic abuse. Additionally, many online resources are available that provide information on how to recognize signs of abuse and how to cope with it. You can also join support groups to connect with others who have experienced similar situations and share your story without fear of judgment or criticism.

No one should have to endure any type of abuse; if you are experiencing narcissistic abuse, know there is hope for healing and recovery. Don't hesitate to reach out for help when you need it most.

Reactive Abuse

Reactive abuse is a term used to describe a specific dynamic that often occurs in narcissistic relationships. This happens when a person who a narcissist is abusing responds to the abuse in a way that may be seen as aggressive or confrontational, and the narcissist uses this response to justify their abusive behavior. Essentially, reactive abuse is how narcissists manipulate their victims and deflect responsibility for their abusive actions. Narcissists can use reactive abuse against you to play the victim and make you out to be the "crazy one" or "abusive one" in the relationship.

The signs of reactive abuse are often subtle and difficult to recognize. Victims may feel like they are walking on eggshells around their abuser or that they must constantly monitor their behavior to avoid triggering them. They may also experience feelings of guilt or shame for reacting aggressively.

It is important to remember that reactive abuse is not the same as mutual abuse. In cases of mutual abuse, both parties engage in abusive behavior toward each other. With reactive abuse, the victim only resorts to abusive behavior as a survival mechanism and does not initiate it first.

Signs of reactive abuse may include:

- Physical aggression, such as hitting or pushing.

- Verbal aggression, such as name-calling or threats.

- Emotional manipulation, such as guilt-tripping or gaslighting.

Victims of reactive abuse should seek help from professionals specializing in narcissistic relationships. There are also resources available online, such as The Hotline, which provides confidential support 24/7/365 for victims of domestic violence and those affected by narcissistic relationships. Additionally, organizations like QueenBeeing provide helpful information and resources about reactive abuse and how to disempower your abuser.

It is important to remember that victims of reactive abuse are not abusers themselves; instead, they respond to an abusive situation out of fear and desperation. If you believe someone you know is a victim of reactive abuse, it is essential to provide them with support and resources so they can get help.

It is also essential to understand that the cycle of narcissistic abuse is intentional and calculated and is designed to maintain control over the victim. Breaking free from this cycle can be difficult, but recognizing the warning signs and seeking support can be an essential first step toward healing and reclaiming one's sense of self-worth and autonomy.

If you think you may be experiencing reactive abuse, it is essential to reach out for help right away so you can get the support you need and start taking steps toward healing from this traumatic experience.

Chapter 4

The Games Narcissists Play

Narcissists often use manipulation, deception, and other tactics to control and dominate those around them. One of the ways they do this is through playing mind games. These games are designed to keep their victims off-balance, confused, and constantly second-guessing themselves. Narcissists often use a variety of manipulation tactics to control their victims. These tactics include gaslighting, love bombing, triangulation, projection, playing the victim, smear campaigns, lying, insinuating comments, discouraging and criticizing others, diminishing and dismissing others' opinions and feelings, making you feel special, and using shock or guilt to manipulate.

It's important to understand that the abuse is not your fault. Narcissists have deep-seated emotional issues that lead them to treat others cruelly. You are not responsible for their behavior, nor can you change them. It's essential to recognize the games and manipulations they play and take steps to protect yourself from them.

Let's explore the different games and forms of emotional manipulation common to many narcissists.

Gaslighting

Gaslighting is a form of psychological manipulation used to gain power and control over another individual. It involves the abuser planting seeds of doubt and confusion in their victim's mind, making them question their reality and sanity. Gaslighting can be subtle or overt, but it always has the same goal: to make the victim feel powerless and unable to trust themselves.

Narcissists often use gaslighting to make their victims feel like they are crazy or wrong for feeling certain emotions or having certain opinions. They may deny things they said or did, make excuses for why they acted a certain way, or even blame the victim for something that was their fault. This manipulation can be highly damaging to the victim's mental health and self-esteem, as it can cause them to doubt themselves and become more dependent on the abuser.

Another way narcissists use gaslighting is by constantly changing the rules of engagement to keep the victim off balance. They may set unrealistic expectations or standards that are impossible to meet, then criticize the victim when they don't meet them. This can create an environment where the victim feels like nothing they do is ever good enough, further weakening their sense of self-worth.

Gaslighting can have long-term effects on a person's mental health, leading to anxiety, depression, low self-esteem, and even suicidal thoughts. It is vital for victims of gaslighting to reach out for help from trusted friends and family members as soon as possible to begin healing from this type of abuse and take steps to empower themselves when being gaslighted.

The first step is to recognize the warning signs of gaslighting. This may include feeling like conversations are circular or unfair or that your perception of reality is being challenged. It may be time to take action if you notice any of these signs in your interactions with someone.

The next step is to practice self-validation and trust your instincts and perceptions. Gaslighters often try to convince you that your reactions are wrong or invalid, but it's important to remember that only you know what's best for yourself.

It's also important to approach the gaslighter directly. Doing so can help you set boundaries and clarify their unacceptable behavior. However, it's essential to remain mindful of your safety when doing this and the safety of those around you.

Finally, focusing on actions rather than words is essential when dealing with a gaslighter. They may tell you what you want to hear to keep you in the relationship, but their actions will speak louder than their words.

These steps can help empower oneself when gaslighted and create a safe space for yourself emotionally and physically. Remember that no one deserves to be manipulated or mistreated, so don't hesitate to take action if needed!

Love Bombing

Love bombing is a form of psychological and emotional manipulation narcissists use to control their victims. It involves showering the victim with excessive attention, affection, and gifts to make them feel dependent on the narcissist. This can be done through grand romantic gestures, compliments, and promises of commitment.

The goal of love bombing is to create an intense bond between the narcissist and their victim that can be difficult for the victim to break away from. The narcissist may use this bond to manipulate their victim into doing things that they want or need them to do.

Some common signs that you may be experiencing love bombing include:

- Excessive flattery or compliments

- Lavishing you with gifts

- Making grand gestures such as declarations of love early on in the relationship

- Wanting to spend all their time with you

- Trying to control your decisions or behavior

- Becoming overly jealous or possessive

- Not respecting your boundaries or personal space

- Putting down your friends and family members

Isolating you from other people in your life

If you are experiencing any of these red flags, protecting yourself and seeking necessary help is important. Love bombing can signify manipulation and emotional abuse, so it's important not to ignore any warning signs.

Here are some tips for protecting yourself from the effects of love bombing:

1. Take time to get to know someone before committing. Love bombers often move quickly in relationships, so get to know someone before making any commitments.

2. Pay attention to red flags. If someone is overly controlling or jealous, this could be a sign that they are love-bombing you.

3. Set boundaries and stick to them. Set clear boundaries with your partner about what behavior is acceptable and what isn't.

4. Seek help if needed. If you think you're being manipulated or abused, don't hesitate to reach out for help from friends, family members, or professionals who can provide support and guidance on how best to protect yourself from further harm.

By following these tips, you can protect yourself from the effects of love bombing and ensure your relationship is based on mutual respect and understanding rather than manipulation and control.

Triangulation

Triangulation is a form of emotional abuse that can occur in any relationship but is especially common in relationships with narcissists. It occurs when the narcissist partner introduces a third person into the two-person romantic relationship without their partner's consent. This can be done to make themselves feel better or to gain control over their partner.

The narcissist may use triangulation to reassure themselves of their partner's affection and devotion and manipulate them into providing what they want. The third person could be anyone from an ex-partner, a mutual friend, a family member, or even a stranger. The narcissist often pits these people against each other, creating a lose-lose situation for all involved.

One sign of triangulation is when someone attempts to distract from the real issue or argument. This could be done by changing the topic of conversation or introducing a new element to the discussion. Another sign is when someone tries to tip the scales of an argument in their favor, such as by exaggerating specific facts or downplaying others. Finally, triangulation can reinforce their sense of superiority over another person by making them feel inferior or less important.

To protect oneself from further manipulation due to triangulation, it is vital to have direct conversations with the person engaging in the behavior and set clear boundaries. Additionally, it is important l to be aware of the tactics used and recognize when they are employed against you. Walking away from the situation can also be a helpful way of avoiding further manipulation.

Having a direct conversation with someone can be difficult, but it doesn't have to be. Here are some steps to help you have a successful conversation:

1. Prepare for the conversation by thinking about what you want to say and how you want to say it. Make sure your language is clear and straightforward so that it is understood.

2. Start the conversation friendly by complimenting them or asking an open-ended question. This will help set the tone for the rest of the conversation.

3. Speak up and make sure your voice is heard. Don't be afraid to express yourself and your feelings honestly and openly.

4. Listen carefully to what the other person has to say and try to understand their point of view. Ask questions if needed, but don't talk over them or interrupt them while they speak.

5. Be direct when discussing the issue, and avoid getting sidetracked by other topics or emotions that may arise during the conversation.

6. End the conversation on a positive note, such as by thanking them for their time or expressing appreciation for their input on the matter discussed.

By following these steps, you can ensure that your direct conversations are productive, respectful, and effective in addressing any issues that need to be discussed between two people!

Projection

Narcissists often use projection as a manipulation tactic to deflect their negative behavior onto someone else. Projection is when people attribute their unacceptable thoughts, feelings, or actions to another person. For example, if a narcissist has done something wrong, they may accuse the other person of doing the same thing to avoid taking responsibility for their actions. This can significantly damage the other person's self-esteem and sense of security.

Narcissists can also use projection to make themselves look better than they are. They may project an image of perfection onto themselves while accusing others of being flawed or inadequate. This allows them to maintain control over the situation and gain admiration from those around them.

Projection can also be used to manipulate and control people. Narcissists often project their negative traits onto someone else to make them feel guilty or ashamed, giving the narcissist power over them. They may also use projection to gaslight someone by denying their reality and making them doubt themselves. For example, if they feel jealous of someone, they may accuse that person of being jealous of them. They may also project their insecurities onto others by accusing them of being insecure or untrustworthy. Additionally, they may project their feelings of inadequacy onto others by accusing them of being inadequate or incompetent.

Narcissistic projection is a dangerous form of manipulation that can have long-lasting effects on those subjected. It is essential to recognize this behavior and take steps to protect yourself from it if you find yourself in a relationship with a narcissist.

Here are some tips for protecting yourself:

1. Recognize the signs of projection. It is essential to be aware of the signs that someone is projecting their feelings onto you, such as accusing you of things they are guilty of or expecting you to act in ways that reflect their emotions.

2. Set boundaries. Setting boundaries and communicating them clearly can help protect yourself from further manipulation due to projection in narcissistic relationships. Tell your partner what behavior is acceptable and unacceptable, and stick to those boundaries even if they try to manipulate you into breaking them.

3. Seek support. Talking with a trusted friend or family member about your experiences to gain perspective and emotional support during difficult times can be helpful.

4. Seek professional help if needed. If you feel overwhelmed by the situation, consider seeking

professional help from a therapist or counselor who can guide how best to handle the situation and protect yourself from further manipulation due to projection in narcissistic relationships.

By being aware of the signs of projection, setting clear boundaries, seeking support, and getting professional help, one can protect oneself from further manipulation due to projection in narcissistic relationships.

Playing The Victim

Narcissists often view themselves as the victim in relationships, even when they are the ones causing harm. This is because they have an inflated sense of self-importance and entitlement and often manipulate people to get what they want. They may also use guilt-tripping or other tactics to make their partner feel bad for not giving them what they want. Narcissists may also play the victim by exaggerating their suffering or portraying themselves as helpless to gain sympathy from others.

This behavior can damage relationships, as it can create a cycle of manipulation and control. It is essential for those in relationships with narcissists to recognize this behavior and take steps to protect themselves from being taken advantage of. This could include setting boundaries, seeking support from friends and family, or seeking professional help.

Smear Campaigns and Flying Monkeys

A smear campaign with a narcissist is a method of damage control they use when they know they have been found out.

It involves spreading lies and misleading information about their victim to make them look unreliable, disgraced, and untrustworthy. Narcissists are obsessed with their image, so this is their way of showing the world what an ideal human being looks like.

When you are the target of a narcissist's smear campaign, it can be a challenging and emotionally draining experience. A smear campaign is an orchestrated effort by the narcissist to discredit and damage your reputation by spreading lies and malicious content about you. It is important to remember that this campaign aims to make you look bad to protect their image.

The first step in dealing with a smear campaign is to remain calm and not take any action that could further escalate the situation. This includes not responding directly to any of the lies or rumors being spread about you. Instead, focus on gathering evidence that proves your innocence and documenting any interactions with the narcissist.

It is also important to pick your battles carefully when dealing with a narcissist's smear campaign. Not every rumor needs to be addressed; it may be best to ignore some. However, if certain rumors are particularly damaging or untrue, taking action to protect your reputation may be necessary.

It is also important to know your truth during this time, as there will likely be times when you start doubting yourself or feeling overwhelmed by all the negative attention directed at you. Remind yourself that what they say about you isn't true, and focus on staying strong in the face of adversity.

Finally, it is essential that you reach out for support from friends and family during this time, as they can provide emotional comfort and help validate your feelings. Talking through what happened can also help put things into perspective, so don't hesitate to ask for help if needed.

Another way narcissists create smear campaigns is through flying monkeys. Flying monkeys are people who a narcissist manipulates to do their bidding. They are often unaware they are being used and tricked into believing the narcissist's lies and false stories. The term "flying monkeys" comes from the classic story of The Wizard of Oz, where the Wicked Witch of the West uses her flying monkeys to carry out her evil deeds. In a narcissistic relationship, flying monkeys can be family members, friends, or even strangers manipulated by the narcissist to spread rumors, hurt someone's reputation, or even physically harm them. Flying monkeys can also isolate someone from their support system or make them feel guilty for not doing what the narcissist wants.

No matter how they are used, flying monkeys can be incredibly damaging and hurtful for the person being targeted by the narcissist. Recognizing when someone is being manipulated by a narcissist and taking steps to protect yourself from their tactics is essential.

Dealing with narcissistic smear campaigns and flying monkeys can be a challenging experience, but by following these tips, you can get through it with grace and strength.

Remember, no matter how hard things get, stay focused on knowing your truth and never forget who you really are!

Lying and False Accusations

Narcissists are known to use manipulation tactics to control and influence others. One of the most common methods they employ is lying and making false accusations as another form of a smear campaign. Lying allows narcissists to gain power over their victims by creating confusion, doubt, and fear. They often use false accusations to discredit their victims or make them feel guilty or ashamed. For example, a narcissist may accuse someone of stealing from them despite no evidence supporting the accusation. This can make the other person feel guilty and powerless, allowing the narcissist to control them. Additionally, narcissists may also lie about their accomplishments to make themselves appear more successful than they actually are. By doing this, they can gain admiration and respect from those around them, which gives them a sense of power and superiority.

False accusations are used to manipulate people into doing something they don't want to do or even believing something that isn't true. Narcissists may also use lies as a form of punishment, such as when they accuse someone of something they didn't do to make them feel bad about themselves.

Degrading, Demeaning, and Criticizing

Narcissists often use demeaning and criticizing as a form of manipulation. This can come in verbal abuse, such as belittling people's accomplishments or skills or telling them they're not worth anything. It can also involve physical forms of degradation, such as humiliation or threats.

By engaging in this type of behavior, narcissists can keep their victims feeling small, insecure, and unable to make decisions for themselves. This gives them control over the person and allows them to dictate how the person should think and act. Additionally, demeaning others also serves to boost the narcissist's ego, enabling them to feel superior and powerful. For example, narcissists may isolate their partner from family and friends to maintain control over them. They may publicly humiliate their partner to make them feel small and powerless. Finally, they may manipulate their partner into doing things against their will to gain power over them.

One of the most important things to do when dealing with verbal abuse is to recognize it for what it is. Verbal abuse includes aggressive language, insults, name-calling, or jokes that make fun of you or your situation. It may also involve more subtle forms of manipulation, such as withholding affection or using silence as punishment. Once you have identified the behavior as verbal abuse, it is essential to set boundaries and let your abuser know that this type of behavior will not be tolerated.

Another key strategy for coping with verbal abuse is to find support from people who understand what you are going through. Talking about your experience with someone in a similar situation can help provide perspective and validation.

Finally, taking care of yourself during this time is important by engaging in activities that bring joy and relaxation into your life. This could include spending time outdoors, reading books, listening to music, or doing something creative like painting or writing poetry. Taking breaks from the situation can help reduce stress and give you the strength and energy to cope with verbal abuse in a relationship.

These manipulative tactics can be devastating, leaving victims feeling confused, powerless, and even traumatized. It's vital for those who a narcissist has manipulated to seek help from a mental health professional to process their feelings and learn how to cope with the trauma they've experienced.

Blame Shifting

Blame shifting is a common tactic narcissists use in relationships to avoid taking responsibility for their actions. It involves deflecting blame onto the other person and making them feel guilty or wrong for something that was not their fault. Narcissists often use this tactic to manipulate and control their partners, as it allows them to maintain power and control in the relationship. Blame shifting can be a form of gaslighting, as it involves twisting reality to benefit the narcissist's agenda. This manipulation of reality can severely impact relationships, leading to guilt, shame, and confusion in the partner being blamed. It is important to recognize when someone is trying to shift blame onto you so that you can take steps to protect yourself and your relationship.

One example of narcissistic blame shifting is when a narcissist does something wrong and then tries to shift the blame onto someone else. They may try to make it seem like the other person was at fault or that they were not responsible for the outcome. Narcissists may also use this tactic to avoid taking responsibility for their own mistakes and shortcomings.

Another example of narcissistic blame shifting is when a narcissist tries to make it seem like someone else's actions, or words are victimizing them. They may try to paint themselves as the victim to gain sympathy or attention from others while deflecting any criticism away from themselves.

Finally, narcissists may use blame-shifting tactics when confronted about their behavior or lies. Instead of owning up to their mistakes, they often try to deflect the conversation away from themselves and onto another person or situation.

This behavior can have serious consequences in both personal and professional relationships.

In personal relationships, narcissistic blame shifting can lead to feelings of guilt and shame in the person being blamed and feelings of anger and resentment towards the narcissist. This can create a cycle of mistrust and emotional manipulation that can be difficult to break out of.

Narcissistic blame-shifting is a damaging behavior that has far-reaching consequences for personal relationships. It is important for those affected by this behavior to recognize it for what it is and take steps to protect themselves from its harmful effects.

Word Salad and Circular Communication

Narcissists often use "word salad" and circular communication to manipulate and confuse their victims in relationships.

Circular conversations are where they will repeat themselves or ask the same questions over and over again without ever getting an answer. This can frustrate the victim as they feel like they are not being heard or understood. Narcissists use word salad and circular communication to control their victims and maintain power in the relationship.

For example, a narcissist might start talking about how their partner didn't appreciate them enough, then switch to talking about how they weren't given enough credit at work, then back to talking about their partner not understanding them. This type of circular discussion can be used to avoid taking responsibility for their actions or feelings and to gaslight their partner into questioning themselves rather than holding the narcissist accountable.

Narcissists commonly use Word salad to manipulate and confuse their victims. It involves stringing together random words and phrases with no apparent connection, making it difficult for the victim to understand what is being said.

For example, a narcissist may say, "I'm not sure why you're so mad; I was just trying to help you with your problem."

This statement could be interpreted in many different ways, leaving the victim confused and unsure how to respond.

Another example of word salad might be, "I don't know why you're so upset; it's not like I did anything wrong." Again, this statement could be interpreted multiple ways, leaving the victim uncertain and manipulated.

Narcissists use the word salad to control their victims by making them feel confused and powerless. It is essential to recognize when someone is using the word salad as a manipulative tactic so that you can protect yourself from being taken advantage of.

It's important to recognize when someone uses word salad and circular conversations to protect yourself from manipulation and emotional abuse. If you find yourself in a relationship with someone who frequently uses this tactic, it's essential to set boundaries and communicate clearly, so you don't get caught up in their manipulative behavior.

Antagonistic Behavior

Narcissists use antagonistic behaviors as emotional manipulation to gain control over their victims. This type of abuse involves tactics such as gaslighting, verbal abuse, and emotional manipulation. Narcissists view all relationships as a struggle for dominance and use these tactics to oppress their victims emotionally.

Antagonism in relationships can manifest itself in many different ways. One example is when one partner consistently puts down the other through verbal or nonverbal communication. This can include name-calling, belittling comments, or even simply rolling their eyes when the other person speaks. Another example of antagonism is when one partner refuses to compromise or cooperate with the other, leading to a breakdown in communication and trust.

Rolling your eyes is an example of a nonverbal form of communication that is considered antagonistic. Rolling your eyes can be seen as dismissive and condescending, leading to frustration and anger in the person being rolled at. It is important to be aware of how our body language communicates our attitudes and emotions, as it can significantly impact how others perceive us.

Finally, some people may be overly critical of their partners and need to give them more credit for their successes or accomplishments. These behaviors can lead to an unhealthy dynamic within a relationship that can be difficult to overcome.

Why Do Narcissists Play Games And Manipulate Those They Love

Narcissists play games and manipulate those they love and care about to gain control, power, and attention. Narcissists can get what they want by playing mind games and manipulating their loved ones while avoiding any feelings of vulnerability or responsibility.

Psychological abuse from narcissists can be a difficult and dangerous situation to navigate. Recognizing the signs of psychological abuse, such as attempts to control, isolate, or frighten you, is important. If you are in an abusive relationship with a narcissist, there are strategies you can use to protect yourself.

First and foremost, setting and sticking to boundaries is vital. Ensure your partner knows what behaviors you will not tolerate and be prepared to enforce those boundaries if necessary. Additionally, building a support system of friends and family who can provide emotional support when needed is essential.

By recognizing the signs of psychological abuse from narcissists and taking steps to protect themselves, narcissistic abuse victims can regain control of their lives. It is essential to be aware of these manipulative tactics to protect yourself against them. If you suspect someone is trying to manipulate you emotionally, setting boundaries and standing up for yourself is essential. Don't be afraid to speak out against emotional abuse or manipulation; don't let anyone take advantage of your kindness or vulnerability.

Chapter 5

Setting Healthy Boundaries

S etting boundaries in a relationship with someone with a narcissistic personality disorder is essential for maintaining healthy relationships. Narcissists have an inflated sense of self-importance and lack empathy, making them difficult to be around. Setting boundaries helps to protect yourself from the narcissist's manipulative behavior and emotional abuse. It allows you to establish clear expectations and limits on how you will be treated to maintain your self-respect and dignity.

Boundaries are important in narcissistic relationships because they help to create a safe space where both parties can express themselves without fear of judgment or manipulation. By setting boundaries, you can also prevent the narcissist from taking advantage of you or using their power over you to control the relationship. Boundaries also help to ensure that the narcissist respects your needs and feelings, allowing for healthier communication between both parties.

It is important to remember that setting boundaries do not mean cutting off all contact with a narcissist; instead, it means limiting how much time and energy you are willing to devote to the relationship. Establishing boundaries is a process that requires patience, understanding, and communication between both parties for it to be successful.

Here are some strategies to help you set and maintain boundaries with a narcissist:

1. Don't justify, explain, or defend yourself. Narcissists often try to manipulate their victims into feeling guilty or ashamed, so it's important not to give them the satisfaction of an explanation.

2. Leave when it doesn't feel healthy. If you are in an unhealthy situation with a narcissist, don't be afraid to leave and take care of yourself first.

3. Decide what you will tolerate and what you won't. Know your limits and ensure the narcissist is also aware of them.

4. Write down what's happening. Keeping track of events can help you stay organized and remember what happened if the situation escalates further down the line.

5. Accept that some people will not respect your boundaries no matter what you do. It's important to remember that even if someone doesn't respect your boundaries, it doesn't mean that they are right or that you deserve mistreatment from them.

6. Set Boundaries For Yourself - Care for yourself first by setting clear boundaries and sticking to them no

matter what the other person does or says.

7. Don't engage in arguments - Arguing with a narcissist is usually futile as they twist words around and never admit fault or wrongdoing, so it's best not to argue with them if possible.

8. Establish clear communication about expectations and needs.

9. Don't allow yourself to be manipulated or taken advantage of.

10. Don't take responsibility for the narcissist's feelings or behavior.

11. Respect your own feelings and opinions, even if they differ from the narcissist's.

12. Set limits on your time with the narcissist, and stick to them.

13. Don't engage in arguments or debates with the narcissist; walk away if necessary.

14. Don't let the narcissist control the conversation; focus on your needs and feelings.

15. Speak up when you feel disrespected or taken advantage of, and don't be afraid to express your

emotions honestly and openly without fear of judgment or criticism from the narcissist.

16. Don't give in to guilt-tripping tactics used by the narcissist; instead, stand firm in your decision-making process, and don't let yourself be swayed by emotional manipulation techniques used by the narcissist to get their way.

17. Take care of yourself first; prioritize self-care activities such as exercise, meditation, journaling, etc., to maintain a healthy balance between taking care of yourself and others in your life (including the narcissistic person).

Communication With A Narcissist

Communicating with a narcissist can be difficult, but it is possible to have healthy communication. Here are some tips for communicating with a narcissist:

1. Set boundaries and stick to them. Make sure the narcissist knows what acceptable and unacceptable behavior is.

2. Be direct and clear when communicating your needs and expectations. Narcissists often use manipulation tactics, so speak, in a way that is not open to interpretation or manipulation.

3. Avoid engaging in arguments or debates with the narcissist, as this will only lead to further conflict and frustration.

4. Remain calm and composed when speaking to the narcissist, even if they become hostile or aggressive. Do not take their words personally; this will only fuel their behavior.

5. Listen carefully and try to understand where the narcissist is coming from before responding or reacting to their statements or actions. This will help you maintain control of the conversation and avoid escalating potential conflicts arising from misunderstanding each other's perspectives or intentions.

6. Avoid giving compliments or positive reinforcement, as this can be seen as an attempt at manipulation by the narcissist, which could lead to further conflict.

7. If necessary, take a break from communication with the narcissist if things become too heated or overwhelming for either party involved to prevent any further escalation of tension between both parties involved in the conversation/interaction/relationship.

Gray Rock Method

The Gray Rock Method is a technique used to deal with toxic people, particularly narcissists. It involves deliberately acting unresponsive or unengaged when interacting with the person to deflect their attempts at manipulation. The idea is that by not giving them anything to work with, they will eventually lose interest and move on.

This method can be helpful for those who are dealing with a difficult person in their life, such as a partner, family member, or coworker. It requires being emotionally non-responsive and boring - almost like a grey rock - so the person cannot use your reactions against you. It involves deliberately acting unresponsive or unengaged so that the person will lose interest in you. Using the Grey Rock Method is essential to remain calm and not respond emotionally to attempts to manipulate you. You should also avoid arguing and focus on being as dull and uninteresting as possible.

Additionally, it is essential to maintain boundaries and not give the person anything they can use against you. Using the Grey Rock Method, you can protect yourself from further abuse while maintaining your safety and peace of mind. This way, you can protect yourself from further abuse while retaining some relationship.

It's important to remember that the Gray Rock Method should only be used as a last resort when all other options have been exhausted. It's best to try and resolve the situation through communication and understanding first. However, if this isn't an option, then using the Gray Rock Method may be necessary to protect yourself from further harm.

To use the Gray Rock Method effectively, it's important to be consistent in your approach. You must remain unresponsive, even if the person tries to provoke you. This means not engaging in arguments or debates, not giving compliments or positive feedback, and not reacting emotionally. Instead of responding directly to their comments or questions, you can acknowledge them without going into detail.

It's also important to remember that the Gray Rock Method isn't about punishing someone for their behavior; it's about protecting yourself from further manipulation and emotional abuse. Using this technique, you can create boundaries and maintain your peace of mind while still respecting the other person.

No Contact

No contact is an important strategy to protect yourself from a narcissist when all else has failed and you have no other connections to the narcissist, such as sharing children. It involves completely cutting off all communication and interaction with the person. This can be difficult, especially if you have been in a relationship with them for a long time, but breaking the cycle of manipulation and abuse they can cause is necessary. No contact means no phone calls, emails, text messages, or any other type of communication. It also means not engaging in activities involving the narcissist, such as attending events or visiting places where they may be present.

No contact should not be done for just a few weeks or months - it should be indefinite. Even if the narcissist has access to ways of contacting you, they will continue to try and manipulate you if you don't take steps to protect yourself. When going no contact with a narcissist, it's essential to avoid making certain mistakes, such as responding to their attempts at communication or giving in to their demands for attention.

The effects of no contact on a narcissist can vary depending on how deeply entrenched they are in their narcissistic behavior. Generally speaking, though, it can lead them into a spiral of toxic behavior such as love bombing and self-victimization. Ultimately, what hurts them most is realizing that you can move on without them and become independent from their presence in your life.

Going No Contact with a Narcissist can be difficult, but protecting yourself from their toxic behavior is a critical step. However, people make mistakes when going to No Contact, making the process more difficult.

Here are 10 mistakes to avoid when going No Contact with a Narcissist:

1. Don't give them any explanation - Giving the narcissist an explanation as to why you are going No Contact will only allow them to manipulate or guilt-trip you into staying in contact with them.

2. Don't respond to their messages - Even if they reach out after you have gone No Contact, don't engage in conversation with them.

3. Don't try to get revenge - Going No Contact is not about getting revenge on the narcissist; it is about protecting yourself from their toxic behavior and taking care of your mental health.

4. Don't expect them to change - Going No Contact will not magically make the narcissist change; they may still try to contact you even after you have gone No Contact. It is essential not to fall back into their manipulative behavior patterns.

5. Don't feel guilty for going No Contact - It can be easy for the narcissist to make you feel guilty for wanting space or time away from them but remember that it is your right and responsibility to take care of yourself first and foremost.

6. Don't underestimate their ability to manipulate - The narcissist may try different tactics such as love-bombing or self-victimization to get what they want, so be aware of these tactics and don't let yourself be manipulated by them again.

7. Remember your support system - Going through this process can be difficult, so make sure you have a strong support system of friends and family who can help you through this time if needed.

8. Remember self-care - Taking care of yourself during this time is essential, so make sure that you eat well, exercise regularly, get enough sleep, etc., to keep your mental health in check.

9. Don't forget why you went No Contact in the first place – Remind yourself of this whenever necessary throughout the process.

10. Don't give up – Going to No Contact with a Narcissist can be challenging, but it is worth it for your well-being; don't give up even if things aren't improving at first!

No contact isn't easy, but it is sometimes necessary if you want to escape the claws of a narcissist and reclaim your life back from them. The length of time before they reach out again varies greatly depending on the individual, but rest assured that eventually, they will come back trying to manipulate you again - so stay strong and remember why you chose this path in the first place!

Chapter 6

The Importance of Self Care

Self-care is an integral part of healing from a narcissistic relationship. It can help survivors to process their experiences, build resilience and create healthy boundaries. Self-care can also provide a sense of safety and security, which is especially important for those who have been in an abusive relationship. It can help survivors to reconnect with themselves and develop a sense of self-worth and identity outside of the relationship. Self-care activities such as journaling, meditation, yoga, exercise, music, hobbies, good nutrition and hydration, art therapy, and spending time with supportive friends and family can all be beneficial in helping survivors heal from the trauma of narcissistic relationships.

Journaling

Journaling can be a powerful tool for those recovering from narcissistic relationships. Writing down experiences can help to process and make sense of difficult emotions while also providing an opportunity to reflect on the past and gain insight into oneself. Journaling can also be used to document evidence of narcissistic abuse, which may be necessary for the healing process.

When journaling about narcissistic relationships, it is essential to focus on both the positive and negative aspects of the experience. Writing down thoughts and feelings related to the relationship can help to identify patterns of behavior that may have been overlooked or ignored during the relationship. This can provide valuable insight into how one has been affected by the narcissist's behavior and how one might better protect themselves in future relationships.

It is also beneficial to use journal prompts when writing about narcissistic relationships. Prompts such as "What signs of narcissistic abuse have you seen and how did they affect you?" or "How did it influence your relationships with others?" can help focus one's writing on specific topics relevant to their experience. Additionally, prompts can provide structure for those unsure of where to start when writing about their experiences with a narcissist.

Overall, journaling about narcissistic relationships can be a helpful tool for recovery and self-reflection. It allows individuals to explore their own emotions and gain insight into their experiences with a narcissist while also helping them build resilience against future toxic relationships.

Here are three ways to get started:

1. Write down your thoughts and feelings about the experience. Journaling is an opportunity to express yourself without judgment, so don't worry about making it perfect or having all the answers.

2. Reflect on what you have learned from the experience. Writing down your observations can help you gain

insight into how you respond to certain situations and how to protect yourself in the future better.

3. Create a timeline of events leading up to and after the experience. This will help you identify patterns in behavior that may have been overlooked before and clarify how far you have come since then.

Journaling is a great way to process difficult emotions and experiences, so don't be afraid to try it!

Meditation

Narcissistic relationships can be incredibly draining and challenging to navigate. Taking care of yourself and practicing self-care during this time is important. One way to do this is through meditation.

Meditation helps us become more aware of our thoughts, feelings, and emotions, allowing us to understand ourselves and our reactions better. This can help us clarify how we feel in a narcissistic relationship and how best to cope. Guided meditations are beneficial as they provide structure and support for the listener.

Guided meditations designed for healing from narcissistic abuse can be particularly beneficial. These meditations often focus on self-acceptance, self-love, and emotional healing. They can also help us to work through unresolved grief after a narcissistic relationship has ended.

Mindfulness meditation involves focusing on the present moment and being aware of your thoughts and feelings without judgment. Guided meditations include listening to an audio recording or following along with a script that helps you focus on relaxation and calming your mind.

Body scans involve paying attention to each part of your body, in turn, to help bring awareness to physical sensations.

Self-care meditations can also be tailored to specific needs or goals. For example, if you're looking for help adapting to your environment, try a 4-minute sacral chakra meditation. If you need extra self-love, there are meditations specifically designed to give you a space to practice loving yourself.

No matter what type of meditation for self-care you choose, it's essential to make it part of your regular routine so that it becomes a habit. Taking just 10 minutes out of your day for self-care can positively affect your mental and physical health.

Yoga and Exercise

Yoga and exercise can be a great form of self-care in narcissistic relationships. Yoga helps to bring balance and peace of mind and body while also providing an opportunity for self-reflection. Exercise can help reduce stress, improve mood, and increase energy levels. Both yoga and exercise can help build resilience against the emotional abuse often present in narcissistic relationships. Practicing yoga can help with many other aspects of life, such as increasing self-awareness, improving communication skills, and developing healthier coping mechanisms. Exercise can also provide an outlet for releasing pent-up emotions or frustrations from the relationship.

There are many different types of exercises to choose from. Popular types of exercises include aerobic, anaerobic, strength training, balance, flexibility, HIIT & Crossfit, Yoga & Pilates, sports training, and recovery.

Aerobic exercise is any activity that increases your heart rate and breathing for an extended period of time. Examples include running, swimming, cycling, or brisk walking. Anaerobic exercise is a type of exercise that requires short bursts of energy, such as sprinting or weight lifting. Strength training helps build muscle and improve overall physical fitness. Balance exercises help improve coordination and stability, while flexibility exercises help keep your muscles limber and reduce the risk of injury.

HIIT & Crossfit are high-intensity interval training workouts that combine cardio with strength training for a full-body workout. Yoga & Pilates focus on stretching and strengthening the body through mindful movements. Sports training can help you improve at a specific sport by improving your agility and speed, while recovery exercises focus on restoring the body after intense physical activity.

Yoga and Pilates are both low-impact exercises that offer numerous health benefits. Yoga and Pilates can help improve flexibility, strength, balance, coordination, posture, and mental clarity. Practicing yoga or Pilates can also reduce stress levels and improve overall well-being.

Yoga is a practice that focuses on breath control, meditation, and poses designed to strengthen the body while calming the mind. It is known for its ability to reduce stress and increase relaxation. Pilates is a form of exercise focusing on core strength, alignment, breathing techniques, and postural awareness. It helps build strength in the abdominal muscles and improve posture and balance.

Both yoga and Pilates can be tailored to suit any fitness level or age group. They are excellent exercises for those looking to improve their physical and mental health. Additionally, they are both low-impact exercises which make them suitable for people with joint issues or injuries who may not be able to participate in more intense exercise such as running or weight lifting.

Yoga and Pilates offer many advantages for those looking to improve their physical and mental health. With regular practice of either yoga or Pilates, you can expect improved flexibility, strength, balance, coordination, posture, stress levels, and overall well-being.

No matter what exercise you choose, listening to your body and taking breaks when needed is essential. Exercising regularly can help boost your mood and energy levels while helping you stay physically and mentally healthy! Taking time for yourself through yoga or exercise is essential in recovering from narcissistic abuse and building a more beneficial relationship with yourself.

Music and Art

Music and art can be powerful tools for self-care. Music has the power to reduce stress and improve cognitive performance, while art provides an outlet for emotional expression.

Music is an integral part of self-care. It can help us relax, reduce stress and anxiety, and even increase our dopamine levels. Listening to music can be a great way to take a break from the hustle and bustle of everyday life and focus on ourselves.

One way to engage with music for self-care is through lyric analysis. This involves listening to a song and thinking about what it means. We can gain insight into our emotions and experiences by breaking down the lyrics. We can also use music as a form of creative expression by writing songs or playing instruments.

Music therapy is another way to use music for self-care. Music therapists are trained professionals who use music in therapeutic settings to help people manage their mental health issues, such as depression or anxiety. They may also use musical activities such as singing, playing instruments, improvisation, or movement exercises to help clients express themselves in a safe environment.

Finally, many other activities involve using music for self-care. These include listening to calming music while meditating or practicing yoga, engaging in musical activities with friends or family members, or simply listening to your favorite songs and enjoying the moment.

No matter how you choose to engage with music for self-care, it's important that you find something that works for you and makes you feel good!

Here are some ways you can add music to your daily routine:

1. Listen to music while you work or study. Listening to music while working or studying can help keep you focused and motivated. It can also help reduce stress levels and make the task more enjoyable.

2. Make a playlist for yourself. Creating a personalized playlist of songs that motivate or inspire you is a great way to get energized for the day ahead. You can also use this playlist as background music while working or studying or as something to listen to during downtime.

3. Take up an instrument. Learning how to play an instrument is fun and provides numerous benefits, such as improved coordination, memory, focus, and creativity. Plus, playing an instrument is a great way to express yourself musically!

4. Attend concerts or live shows. Going out and experiencing live music is a great way to appreciate different genres of music and connect with other people who share similar interests in music as you do!

5. Sing along with your favorite songs! Singing along with your favorite songs is not only fun, but it also helps boost self-confidence and lift spirits! So don't be afraid to belt out those tunes whenever you feel like it!

Art can be another important part of self-care. Engaging with art can help us to express our emotions, embrace mistakes, foster self-compassion, and connect with others. It can be a great way to relax and take a break from everyday life.

Creating art can be a powerful tool for self-care. It helps us to accept and explore our feelings, soothe our minds, and feed our souls. Art therapy exercises such as creating a safe space, coloring a feeling wheel, or making response art are all great ways to practice self-care through creative expression.

Artists often use creating as an outlet to channel their anxieties or process trauma through sharing and storytelling. Even if you don't consider yourself an artist, engaging in arts and crafts is still beneficial for your well-being. Making time for art can help you relax and unwind while allowing you to express yourself in new ways.

No matter your skill level or ability, engaging with art can be an excellent form of self-care. So why not give it a try? You might find that it's the perfect addition to your routine!

Here are some ideas for how to incorporate art into your daily routine:

1. Take up an old hobby or learn a new one - Whether it's painting, drawing, sculpting, or something else entirely, dedicating time each day to a creative activity can help you stay inspired and motivated.

2. Take pictures of interesting things - Photography is a great way to capture the beauty of the world around you and uniquely express yourself.

3. Get lost in a good book - Reading is an excellent way to stimulate your imagination and explore different perspectives on life.

4. Go to an independent movie theater - Watching films can inspire and provide insight into different cultures and lifestyles.

5. Find art events in your area - Attending local art shows, exhibitions, or performances can be a great way to get exposed to new ideas and connect with other creatives in your community.

6. Make a list of everything that can be cut from your daily routine that isn't improving your life - This will give you more time for creative activities without sacrificing anything important from your schedule.

7. Use that extra time to create something meaningful - Whether it's writing poetry, composing music, or creating visual art, use this newfound free time as an opportunity to make something unique that expresses who you are as an artist.

8. Partaking in different art expressions - From dance classes to pottery-making workshops, there are plenty of ways to explore various forms of artistic expression and find what resonates with you most deeply.

9. Incorporate art into home décor - Decorating with artwork is not only aesthetically pleasing but also helps bring positive energy into the home

environment while expressing personal style at the same time.

10. Create a daily art habit- Setting aside regular times throughout the day for creative activities such as sketching or doodling can help cultivate an artistic mindset over time and make creating part of your everyday life!

By engaging in music and art activities as part of self-care, you can gain insight into better managing your narcissistic relationship.

Nutrition

Good nutrition is an essential part of self-care. Eating a balanced diet with lean meats, poultry, legumes, nuts, seeds, whole grains, dairy, and healthy fats can help to nourish your body and mind. Taking the time to cook nutritious meals can be a great way to practice self-care. Not only will you nourish your body with the proper nutrients, but you can also take the time to enjoy the process of cooking and eating without distractions such as phones or television.

It's also important to pay attention to how food makes you feel physically and emotionally. Eating foods that make you feel energized and satisfied can help promote positive feelings towards yourself and your relationship with food. Additionally, ensuring that you are getting enough fruits and vegetables in your diet can provide essential vitamins, minerals, fiber, and antioxidants that are all beneficial for overall health.

Snacking can be a great way to get the nutrition your body needs throughout the day. However, it's important to make sure you choose healthy snacks to help you reach your health goals. Here are some tips for eating healthy snacks:

1. Choose snacks with protein and fiber. Protein and fiber are essential nutrients for keeping you full and satisfied between meals. Look for protein and fiber snacks, such as nuts, seeds, yogurt, or whole grain crackers.

2. Avoid processed foods. Processed foods often contain added sugars and unhealthy fats that can lead to weight gain over time. Instead, choose fresh fruits and vegetables or minimally processed snacks like air-popped popcorn or homemade trail mix.

3. Read nutrition labels carefully. Nutrition labels can help you identify which snacks are healthier than others by providing information about calories, fat content, sugar content, and other nutrients in each serving size.

4. Keep portion sizes in check. Even healthy snacks can be high in calories if eaten in large portions, so be mindful of how much you consume at once!

5. Make snacking part of a balanced diet overall. Snacks should make up no more than 20-25% of your daily calorie intake; the rest should come from nutrient-dense meals that include lean proteins, whole grains, fruits and vegetables, and healthy fats like olive oil or avocado oil.

By following these tips for eating healthy snacks, you'll be able to enjoy delicious treats while still reaching your health goals!

If you're looking for a healthy snack between meals, plenty of delicious options are available. From roasted chickpeas and hummus to air-fried snacks and protein chips, many nutritious snacks can help you stay full and energized throughout the day.

For example, Quest Nutrition Tortilla Style Protein Chips, Chili Lime, and Baked are excellent options for crunchy snacks. These chips are high in protein and low in fat, making them an ideal snack for those trying to lose weight.

Another great option is Evolved Chocolate Hazelnut Flavored Keto Cups. These cups provide a sweet treat without all the sugar and calories of traditional desserts. They're also packed with healthy fats that help keep you full longer.

Finally, North Sea Fish Snacks are an excellent source of omega-3 fatty acids that can help reduce inflammation and improve heart health. Plus, they're low in calories and make a great alternative to potato chips or other unhealthy snacks.

No matter what type of snack you're looking for, there's something out there that will satisfy your cravings while still being good for your health. With so many healthy options available, it's easy to find something that fits your dietary needs and tastes great too!

Finally, it's important to remember that self-care isn't just about what we eat but also how we eat it. Taking the time to savor each bite of food while eating slowly can help us appreciate our meals more fully and recognize when we are full faster.

Overall, good nutrition is an essential part of self-care as it helps us nourish our bodies with the proper nutrients while also allowing us to practice mindful eating habits.

Drinking water is also an essential part of self-care. Staying hydrated helps to keep your body functioning properly and can even help you feel more energized and alert. Drinking enough water can also help with digestion, skin health, and overall well-being.

Knowing how much water you should be drinking each day is essential. Generally speaking, adults need about four to six cups of water per day, but this amount varies depending on activity level and other factors. It's also important to note that not all fluids count towards your daily intake - caffeinated beverages like coffee or tea don't provide the same benefits as plain water.

Here are some tips for drinking more water during the day:

1. Carry a reusable water bottle with you throughout the day and refill it regularly.

2. Add flavor to your water by infusing it with fruits or herbs like mint or cucumber.

Set reminders on your phone or watch to remind yourself to drink more water throughout the day.

4. Drink a glass of water before each meal and snack as part of your routine.

5. When thirsty, choose sparkling or flavored waters instead of sugary drinks like soda or juice.

6. Eat foods with high-water content, such as cucumbers, celery, tomatoes, melons, and oranges, to help increase your fluid intake without having to drink extra glasses of water daily.

7. Freeze some freezer-safe bottles, so you always have cold water ready when you need it.

8. Use an app like WaterMinder to track how much you've been drinking throughout the day and set goals for yourself if needed!

Taking care of yourself includes ensuring you get enough fluids daily. Drinking plenty of water is an easy way to ensure your body has what it needs for optimal health and well-being.

Hobbies

Hobbies can be a great way to practice self-care. Engaging in activities that bring you joy can help reduce stress and improve your overall well-being. From puzzles and crafts to music and nature walks, plenty of hobbies can help you relax and restore your energy.

Creative hobbies such as knitting, crocheting, scrapbooking, painting, or drawing can be especially beneficial for self-care. Not only do they provide an outlet for expression, but they also allow you to focus on something other than the stressors in your life.

If you're looking for something more active, consider taking up a sport or joining a club. Playing sports or engaging in group activities can help boost your mood and allow you to socialize with others.

Here are ideas on hobbies that can help you practice self-care:

1. Meditation and yoga can help reduce stress, improve focus, and increase mindfulness.

2. Cooking - learning how to cook can be a great way to relax and enjoy yourself while nourishing your body with healthy meals.

3. Playing puzzles

4. Artwork - explore different mediums such as painting, drawing, or sculpting.

5. Learning a new language

Take a long walk, go on a nature hike, or ride a bike.

7. Do some gardening or plant something new, start an herb garden

8. Take up Knitting, crocheting,

9. Scrapbooking

10. Spending time outdoors in nature

11. Engage in a new sport on an old sport you used to enjoy. Join a community league.

12. Join a book club

13. Find a volunteer organization to get involved with

No matter what hobby you choose, it's important to make sure it's something that brings you joy and relaxation. Taking time out of your day to focus on yourself is essential for maintaining good mental health. So why not try something new today?

Your Tribe Is Your Vibe

A strong support system can help reduce stress, provide emotional support, and give you a sense of belonging. Your Tribe is your Vibe!

Having supportive people can help you feel less alone when facing difficult times. They can offer advice or just be there to listen without judgment. Spending time with them can also be a great way to take your mind off stressful situations and have fun. Whether going out for dinner, playing board games or just talking about life, having quality time with loved ones can benefit your mental health.

Here are some tips to help you nurture your relationships:

1. Communication is key - make sure to talk openly and honestly with your partner about any issues or concerns that arise.

2. Show appreciation for the other person - let them know how much they mean to you and how much you value their presence in your life.

3. Spend quality time together - take the time to do activities together, whether going out for dinner or just watching a movie at home.

4. Be compassionate and understanding - try to put yourself in the other person's shoes and be understanding of their feelings and emotions.

5. Forgive each other - no one is perfect, so it's essential to learn how to forgive each other when mistakes are made.

6. Create rituals together - find something special you enjoy doing together, such as cooking a meal or

walking in the park on Sunday mornings.

7. Balance social and alone time - while it's important to spend quality time together, it's also essential to have some alone time so that each person can recharge and focus on themselves occasionally.

Healing from a narcissistic relationship can be arduous, but self-care is an important part of the journey. Self-care involves taking time to focus on your feelings and emotional experience, recognizing your wants and needs, and gently nurturing yourself. It also involves setting boundaries with the narcissist to protect yourself from further harm. Additionally, it is essential to remember why the relationship needed to end and accept that closure cannot come from the narcissist - it must come from within. Taking care of yourself is key to recovering from narcissistic abuse and will help you move forward.

Chapter 7

Techniques to Calm Anxiety

motional Regulation

E When dealing with a narcissist, emotional regulation is an essential tool to have in your arsenal. Emotional regulation can help you manage complex emotions when interacting with a narcissist, such as anger, frustration, and sadness. It can also help you stay calm and focused on the task rather than overwhelmed by the narcissist's manipulative tactics. By understanding how to regulate your emotions in these situations, you can better protect yourself from being taken advantage of by a narcissist.

Narcissists often use people as emotional regulators to control their feelings and reactions. They may try to manipulate you into feeling certain emotions so that they can feel better about themselves or gain something from the situation. This unhealthy behavior can lead to further distress for both parties involved. Therefore, it is vital to be aware of this dynamic and take steps to protect yourself from it.

One way to do this is by learning to recognize your emotions and practicing healthy coping strategies when dealing with a narcissist. This includes setting boundaries and limits on what behaviors are acceptable in the relationship and taking time for self-care activities like meditation or journaling that will help you stay grounded during challenging interactions. Additionally, it is essential to remember that no matter how hard a narcissist may try to make you feel bad about yourself or manipulate you into doing something against your will, ultimately, it is up to you how you choose to respond in any given situation.

It can be challenging to learn how to regulate your emotions, but it's possible with the right tips and strategies. Here are nine tips for emotional regulation that can help you manage your feelings more effectively:

1. Know what your go-to numbing behaviors are. Identifying these behaviors can help you avoid them in the future.

2. Start with identifying your feelings. Taking the time to understand what you're feeling can help you better manage those emotions.

3. Resist judging your feelings. Don't be too hard on yourself regarding how you feel – acknowledge them and move on.

4. Ask yourself, "What are my needs?" Understanding what you need to feel better can help you find ways to meet those needs and regulate your emotions more effectively.

5.

Recognize your emotion and validate your feelings. Acknowledging your feelings is an essential step in managing those emotions more effectively.

6. Consider riding it out rather than trying to suppress or ignore the emotion altogether – this will give you time to process what's going on and devise a plan of action if needed.

7. Try self-soothing techniques such as deep breathing, meditation, or journaling to calm down and regain a regulated state of mind quickly after experiencing strong emotions or stressors in life.

8. Practice mindfulness by focusing on the present rather than worrying about the past or future – this can help reduce stress levels and improve emotional regulation skills over time and provide clarity on how best to handle certain situations or emotions that arise throughout the day/week/month etc...

9. Learn Cognitive Behavioral Therapy (CBT) skills such as challenging negative thoughts, reframing situations, problem-solving, etc., which can all be used as tools for managing difficult emotions more effectively when they arise in life situations or everyday interactions with others around us.

By practicing emotional regulation when dealing with a narcissist, we can better protect ourselves from being taken advantage of while maintaining our sense of self-worth and dignity.

Guided Meditation

Anxiety can be overwhelming and challenging to manage, but it doesn't have to be. Guided meditation is a powerful tool for relaxation and inner peace. It can help reduce stress, anxiety, depression, and negative emotions while increasing self-awareness and mindfulness. Studies have shown that guided meditation can lower blood pressure, improve symptoms of irritable bowel syndrome, reduce insomnia, and even help people with substance abuse issues. It can also help to lengthen attention span and increase focus.

The key to experiencing the benefits of guided meditation is to practice regularly. Taking time out of your day to sit quietly and focus on your breath or a mantra can be incredibly calming and restorative. With practice, you will better manage stress in daily life and gain greater insight into yourself.

If you're new to guided meditation, find a teacher or program that resonates with you to get the most out of your practice. Many types of guided meditations are available online or through apps that offer audio recordings or video tutorials from experienced teachers.

The benefits are undeniable regardless of the type of guided meditation you choose. Taking time for yourself each day to relax and connect with your inner self can make a huge difference in how you feel mentally and physically.

Simple Guided Meditation Practice

Here is a simple guided meditation to help you reduce anxiety and find inner calm.

Start by finding a comfortable place to sit or lie down. Close your eyes and take a few deep breaths, focusing on each inhalation and exhalation. As you inhale, imagine all the tension in your body melting away with each breath. As you exhale, imagine releasing any worries or anxieties weighing on your mind.

Now bring your attention to your heart center. Visualize a warm, golden light radiating from your chest, filling every corner of your body with warmth and healing energy. Feel the light soothing away any physical discomfort or emotional distress that you may be feeling.

Take some time to explore this feeling of relaxation and peace as it spreads throughout your body. Notice how it feels to let go of any anxious thoughts or worries that may have held you back from living fully in the present moment.

When you are ready, slowly open your eyes and take one last deep breath before returning to the world around you. Remember that this feeling of calm is always within reach whenever you need it - all it takes is a few moments of mindful awareness and relaxation to access it again.

4-Minute Sacral Chakra Meditation

Sacral chakra meditation is a great way to bring balance and harmony to your body and mind. The sacral chakra is located in the lower abdomen and is associated with creativity, pleasure, and emotions. A 4-minute sacral chakra meditation can help you relax, open your creative energy, and connect with your emotions.

To start your 4-minute sacral chakra meditation, find a comfortable place to sit or lie down. Close your eyes and take a few deep breaths. As you inhale deeply through your nose, feel the air entering and expanding your lungs. Feel the tension leaving your body as you exhale slowly through your mouth.

Now focus on the area around your lower abdomen where the sacral chakra is located. Visualize a bright orange light radiating from this area of your body. Feel its warmth as it spreads throughout your body, calming any tension or stress you may feel.

As you continue to meditate on this orange light, imagine it connecting with all of the other areas of your body that need healing or balance. Allow yourself to be fully immersed in this visualization for the remainder of the 4 minutes. When you're finished, take a few more deep breaths before opening your eyes and returning to reality.

Practicing a 4-minute sacral chakra meditation can bring balance and harmony into all aspects of life. It can also help reduce stress levels while increasing creativity and emotional awareness. Give it a try today!

Simple Breathing Exercise

If you're feeling anxious, try this simple breathing exercise to help you relax.

Find a comfortable position, either sitting or lying down, and close your eyes.

2. Take a deep breath in through your nose for four seconds, feeling the air fill your lungs.

3. Hold your breath for seven seconds, allowing yourself to feel the tension slowly dissipate.

4. Exhale slowly through your mouth for eight seconds, making a whooshing sound as you release all the air from your lungs.

5. Repeat this cycle several times until you feel calm and relaxed.

Breathing exercises can be an effective way to reduce stress and anxiety in moments of distress or panic. Taking slow, deep breaths helps to activate the body's natural relaxation response, calming both mind and body while restoring balance and focus. With practice, these techniques can become second nature so that when anxiety arises, you can quickly return to a state of calmness and clarity.

Paced Breathing

Paced breathing is a simple yet effective technique for calming the mind and body. It involves taking slow, deliberate breaths in and out for a specific period of time. The goal is to take deep breaths that fill your lungs completely and then exhale slowly. This type of breathing helps to reduce stress, improve focus, and promote relaxation.

To practice paced breathing, start by standing or sitting comfortably with your feet flat on the floor. Take a deep breath in through your nose while raising your arms slowly over your head. Exhale as you lower your arms back down to your sides. Repeat this process three times.

You can also try other breathing exercises such as "breathing breaks" or "4-7-8 breathing," which involve inhaling for four seconds, holding the breath for seven seconds, and exhaling for eight seconds. These techniques can help you relax and manage anxiety levels.

It's important to note that paced breathing should be done in moderation and not used as a substitute for medical treatment if needed. If you're feeling overly anxious or stressed, it's best to seek professional help from a healthcare provider or mental health specialist.

Progressive Muscle Relaxation

Take a deep breath in, and feel your body relax as you exhale. Starting with your feet, tense the muscles in your feet and hold for five to ten seconds. Then while you exhale, release the tension and feel yourself relaxing.

Move up to your calves and repeat the same process of tensing and releasing the muscles. Continue this process through your legs, hips, abdomen, chest, arms, hands, neck, jaw, and face.

When you reach your face, take another deep breath in again, tense the muscles in the face, and hold this position for a few seconds. Now release. Feel yourself relaxing as you exhale.

Now that your body is relaxed, take one more deep breath in and out slowly. Feel yourself becoming more open with each breath. Enjoy this feeling of relaxation for a few moments before returning to your day.

Visualization

Visualization is a powerful technique that can help reduce the symptoms of anxiety. It involves using mental imagery to create a peaceful and calming environment in your mind. Here are some visualization exercises you can use to calm your anxious mind:

1. Double-paned window technique: Imagine yourself standing in front of a double-paned window, with one pane representing your current state of anxiety and the other pane representing a calmer, more relaxed version of yourself. As you focus on the two panes, imagine the anxious feelings slowly fading away as they move from one pane to the other.

2. Serene beach scene technique: Visualize yourself at a tranquil beach, feeling the sun's warmth on your skin and listening to the sound of waves crashing against the shore. Imagine breathing in deeply and exhaling slowly as you take in this peaceful environment.

3. Stop sign technique: Picture a stop sign in front of you and imagine all your anxious thoughts stopping as soon as they reach it. Feel yourself becoming calmer

and more relaxed with each passing moment as these thoughts dissipate away into nothingness.

4. Blue light technique: Visualize a blue light surrounding you, filling up all space around you with its calming energy until everything else fades away into oblivion, and all that's left is peace and tranquility within you.

5. Ball of yarn technique: Imagine holding onto a ball of yarn that represents all your worries and anxieties, then slowly unraveling it until nothing is left but an empty string in your hands. Feel yourself becoming lighter and more relaxed with each strand that unravels from the ball of yarn until there's nothing left but peace inside you.

Taking time out for these visualization exercises can help reduce your anxiety levels and find inner peace within yourself.

Grounding 5-4-3-2-1

The 54321 grounding exercise is a great way to manage anxiety and stay focused in the present moment. It involves using your five senses to take in the details of your surroundings and distract yourself from anxious thoughts.

To do this exercise, start by focusing on five things you can see around you. Then move on to four things you can feel, three things you can hear, two things you can smell, and one thing you can taste. This will help ground you in the present moment and distract you from anxious thoughts.

Temperature

Temperature is used to help regulate our physiology when we are feeling overwhelmed or distressed. This can be done by exposing our face to cold water or holding an ice pack on our neck or forehead. This temperature helps to calm down quickly and reduces extreme emotion. Hot objects such as a warm bath or shower can be used to relax the body and reduce feelings of anxiety or stress.

It is important to remember that temperature regulation should only be used as a short-term solution, not as a substitute for other coping strategies, such as mindfulness, self-soothing, and problem-solving. It should also not be used if it could cause harm to yourself or others.

The Butterfly Hug

The butterfly hug is an easy relaxation technique that can be used anytime, anywhere to help with anxiety, stress, and feeling overwhelmed. EMDR therapists created it to help children in the aftermath of a natural disaster in Mexico City in 1998.

The butterfly hug involves crossing your hands across your chest, with your middle fingers resting on your collarbones. Then, raise your elbows to level with your shoulders, and take a few deep breaths. This helps to calm the senses and relax the muscles. You can also add visualization techniques, such as imagining yourself surrounded by a calming color or light.

***

It's important to remember that these exercises may not work for everyone, but it is worth trying if you are feeling overwhelmed with anxiety or panic attacks. Focus on the ones that work best for you. Think of them as mental tools, find as many that are helpful for you, and then file them away in your mental toolbox to take out and use as needed. Additionally, it's important to practice self-care during times of distress and reach out for help if needed.

Chapter 8

Finding The Right Therapist

I often tell people that finding the right therapist or therapeutic modality is like finding the right pair of shoes. Sometimes you must try on a few pairs of shoes before finding the right fit. Finding the right therapist can be similar; not every therapist or therapeutic modality will be the right fit for you. If you find working with a therapist not an excellent fit for you, switching and trying a new one is okay. Keep searching until you find someone you feel you connect well with and in a therapy modality that aligns with your needs.

Finding the right therapist for narcissistic abuse can be difficult for some. It is essential to find someone who understands the complexities of this type of abuse and is experienced in helping people recover. Here are some tips to help you find the right counselor for your needs:

1. Look for a therapist who specializes in narcissistic abuse recovery. This type of therapist will have experience dealing with narcissistic abuse issues and be better equipped to help you heal from the trauma.

2.

Ensure your therapist is covered by your insurance company, if applicable. This will make it easier and more affordable to receive treatment.

3. Ask questions about their experience treating narcissistic abuse victims and how they approach treatment. You want to ensure that they understand the unique challenges associated with this type of trauma and have a plan to help you heal.

4. Find out if they offer additional services, such as group therapy or support groups, that could benefit your recovery process.

5. Make sure that you feel comfortable with your therapist and that they provide an environment where you can feel safe discussing your experiences without judgment or criticism.

6. Finally, look for reviews online from other clients who have seen the same therapist to get an idea of their experience before committing to treatment with them.

The Different Types of Mental Health Doctors, Counselors and Providers

Mental health providers can come in many forms, including psychiatrists, psychologists, licensed clinical social workers, counselors, certified alcohol and drug abuse counselors, nurse psychotherapists, and marital and family therapists. Each of these professionals has unique skills and qualifications that can help individuals with mental health issues.

Psychiatrists are medical doctors who specialize in diagnosing and treating mental illnesses. They can prescribe medications to treat mental health conditions. Psychologists have a doctoral degrees in psychology and are trained to assess and diagnose mental illnesses. They often provide therapy or counseling services for individuals with mental health issues.

Licensed clinical social workers (LCSWs) are trained to provide counseling services for individuals with mental health issues. They also offer case management services to help people access the resources they need for recovery. Counselors (LPCs) typically have a master's degree in counseling or a related field and provide individual or group therapy sessions for those with mental illness.

Certified alcohol and drug abuse counselors (CADCs) specialize in helping people who struggle with substance use disorders. They provide individualized treatment plans focusing on assisting clients in managing their addiction while improving their overall well-being. Nurse psychotherapists (NPs) specialize in providing psychological care to patients with mental illness or emotional distress. Lastly, marital and family therapists (MFTs) work with couples or families to address relationship issues contributing to an individual's mental health struggles.

Overall, many professionals are available to help those struggling with mental health issues find the support they need. It is vital to research different types of providers before deciding which one is right for you or your loved one's needs.

Different Types of Therapeutic Modalities

When choosing the right type of mental health therapy for you, it is important to consider your individual needs and goals. It is also essential to speak with a qualified professional who can help you decide which type of treatment will be most effective for your situation. Psychotherapy is often the first line of treatment for mental health issues as it focuses on understanding the underlying causes of symptoms and helping individuals develop coping strategies.

No matter what type of mental health treatment you choose, it is important that you feel comfortable with your therapist and trust them enough to open up about your struggles without fear of judgment. Below are some common types of psychotherapy modalities and how they can potentially be helpful for you.

Cognitive Behavioral Therapy (CBT)

Cognitive Behavioral Therapy (CBT) is a form of psychotherapy that helps individuals identify and change negative thought patterns and behaviors. It treats various mental health issues, including narcissistic abuse recovery. CBT focuses on the connection between thoughts, feelings, and behaviors. By recognizing the patterns of thinking that lead to certain emotions or behaviors, an individual can learn to modify their responses to better cope with difficult situations.

In the context of narcissistic abuse recovery, CBT can help individuals recognize the patterns of thinking contributing to their suffering. Through this recognition, they can challenge these thoughts and replace them with positive ones. Additionally, CBT can help individuals develop healthier coping mechanisms for dealing with difficult emotions or situations. This could include learning how to set boundaries in relationships or developing strategies for self-care.

Cognitive Behavioral Therapy is an effective tool for helping individuals recover from narcissistic abuse by giving them the skills to manage their thoughts and behaviors healthily. With the proper guidance and support, it can be an invaluable resource in healing from narcissistic abuse.

Acceptance and Commitment Therapy (ACT)

Acceptance and Commitment Therapy (ACT) is a type of psychotherapy that helps individuals accept their thoughts and feelings while committing to action toward their values. It encourages people to embrace their emotions rather than try to eliminate them. This type of therapy can be beneficial in narcissistic abuse recovery as it can help individuals recognize the abuse's impact on their lives, accept it, and move forward healthily.ACT focuses on assisting individuals to become aware of the present moment and how they feel without judgment or criticism. It encourages them to identify what is important to them and commit to taking action toward those values, even if it means facing difficult emotions or situations. This type of therapy also helps individuals develop mindfulness skills better to manage their feelings and reactions in challenging situations.

By learning how to accept difficult emotions, individuals can begin to heal from narcissistic abuse by recognizing its impact on their lives and understanding that they do not have control over what happened in the past. ACT also helps individuals develop healthier coping strategies for dealing with difficult emotions such as anxiety or depression that may arise from the trauma of narcissistic abuse.

Acceptance and Commitment Therapy is an effective form of psychotherapy that can help individuals who have experienced narcissistic abuse recover by teaching them how to accept their thoughts and feelings while committing to action toward their values. By developing mindfulness skills, they can better manage their emotions and reactions in challenging situations, which will ultimately help them heal from the trauma of narcissistic abuse.

Dialectical behavior therapy (DBT)

Dialectical Behavior Therapy (DBT) is a type of cognitive-behavioral therapy that combines strategies like mindfulness, acceptance, and problem-solving to help individuals manage their emotions and behaviors. DBT is particularly helpful in treating narcissistic abuse recovery. It helps individuals learn how to identify and regulate their emotions, as well as how to communicate with others effectively. It teaches distress tolerance, emotional regulation, interpersonal effectiveness, and mindfulness. These skills can help individuals cope with the trauma of narcissistic abuse by providing them with tools to manage their emotions and relationships better. DBT can also help individuals develop healthier coping mechanisms for dealing with the stress of the situation. By learning these skills, individuals can gain greater insight into themselves and their relationships, allowing them to make more informed decisions about how they want to move forward in life.

Mindfulness Therapy

Mindfulness therapy is an evidence-based practice that helps individuals become more aware of their thoughts, feelings, and behaviors to gain insight into their experiences. It is a form of psychotherapy that focuses on the present moment and encourages individuals to observe their thoughts and emotions without judgment. Mindfulness therapy is beneficial for those recovering from narcissistic abuse, as it can help them to understand their reactions and responses to the abuse they have experienced.

Mindfulness therapy helps individuals recognize patterns of thinking that may contribute to their distress, such as rumination or catastrophizing. It also teaches individuals how to respond more effectively when faced with difficult situations or triggers related to the abuse they have experienced. Additionally, mindfulness can help individuals become more aware of how their bodies respond to stressors to manage better physical symptoms associated with traumatic experiences.

Mindfulness therapy can be an effective tool for those recovering from narcissistic abuse by helping them gain insight into their experiences and develop healthier coping strategies for managing difficult emotions or situations.

EMDR Therapy

EMDR, or Eye Movement Desensitization and Reprocessing, is a form of psychotherapy that helps people process and heal from traumatic experiences. It is based on the idea that when we experience trauma, our brains become overwhelmed and unable to process the event healthily. EMDR works by using bilateral stimulation (such as eye movements, tapping, or sound) to help the brain reprocess the traumatic memory and move it into a more adaptive place in the brain. This can help reduce symptoms of anxiety, depression, PTSD, and more.

Regarding narcissistic abuse recovery, EMDR can be particularly helpful in helping survivors process their trauma and move forward with their lives. By allowing them to safely revisit their traumatic memories while being supported by a therapist, they can understand what happened to them and gain insight into how it has impacted their lives. Additionally, EMDR can help survivors learn how to regulate their emotions better and develop healthier coping skills for dealing with triggers related to the abuse. Ultimately, EMDR can give survivors the tools to heal from narcissistic abuse and reclaim their power over their lives.

Somatic Therapy

Somatic therapy is a form of body-centered therapy that looks at the connection between mind and body and uses psychotherapy and physical techniques to help people recover from traumatic experiences, such as narcissistic abuse. It is based on the understanding that trauma can be stored in the body and that we can begin to heal by addressing the physical sensations associated with it.

Somatic therapy works by helping people become aware of their bodies and how they are feeling in the present moment. Through this awareness, they can identify patterns of tension or discomfort that may be linked to past trauma. They can then use various somatic interventions such as breathing exercises, mindfulness practices, movement therapies, and other body-based techniques to release these patterns of tension and return to a state of balance.

By working through these physical sensations in a safe environment with a trained therapist, individuals can gain insight into their own experiences of narcissistic abuse and learn how to manage their emotions better. This process can help them develop healthier coping mechanisms for dealing with difficult situations in the future.

Somatic therapy is an effective tool for those who have experienced narcissistic abuse as it helps them reconnect with their bodies and learn how to trust themselves again. It provides a safe space for healing from trauma while also allowing individuals to gain insight into their own experiences to move forward in life more confidently.

Internal Family Systems (IFS)

Internal Family Systems (IFS) is a therapy that helps individuals address and heal from the effects of narcissistic abuse. It is based on the idea that we all have multiple parts or sub-personalities within us, which can cause internal conflict. IFS works to help people identify, understand, and work with these parts to resolve conflicts and achieve healing.

The IFS model was developed by Richard C. Schwartz in the 1980s and has since become an evidence-based approach to psychotherapy. It focuses on helping people recognize their inner strengths and resources and how their parts interact with each other. By understanding how these parts interact, individuals can learn how to better manage their emotions, thoughts, and behaviors to cope with difficult situations and experiences.

Regarding narcissistic abuse recovery, IFS can be particularly helpful because it provides a safe space for individuals to explore their feelings without judgment or criticism. It also helps them understand why they may feel certain emotions or engage in certain behaviors. This understanding can lead to healthier coping strategies that allow them to move forward in their recovery journey.

Internal Family Systems are a practical therapeutic approach for those looking for help with narcissistic abuse recovery. By recognizing our inner strengths and resources, we can better understand ourselves and our relationships with others to move forward positively.

Alternative Forms of Therapy

Massage Therapy

Massage therapy is a form of healing that involves manipulating the body's soft tissues. It can help manage a health condition or enhance wellness and is particularly beneficial for those recovering from narcissistic abuse. Massage therapy helps to reduce stress, improve circulation, and increase relaxation. It can also help to reduce pain and tension in the body, which can be especially helpful for those who have experienced trauma. Additionally, massage therapy can help to promote emotional healing by providing an opportunity for self-care and connection with a therapist. Through massage therapy, individuals can learn how to relax and care for themselves in a safe environment. This can be especially beneficial for those recovering from narcissistic abuse as it allows them to focus on their needs without feeling overwhelmed or judged. Massage therapy effectively promotes physical and emotional healing while providing an opportunity for self-care and relaxation.

Reiki

Reiki therapy is an ancient healing practice that uses energy to promote relaxation and well-being. It is based on the belief that a universal life force energy flows through all living things, and when this energy is blocked or out of balance, it can lead to physical and emotional issues. Reiki therapy works to restore balance in the body by channeling this life force energy into areas where it is needed most.

Reiki therapy is beneficial for those recovering from narcissistic abuse. Narcissistic abuse can leave victims feeling drained and disconnected from their sense of self-worth. Reiki helps to restore balance and bring back a sense of peace, allowing victims to reconnect with their true selves and find inner strength. The calming effects of Reiki also help reduce stress levels, which can be beneficial for those who have experienced trauma due to narcissistic abuse.

Reiki practitioners use techniques like light touch, hand placements, visualization, and meditation to help facilitate healing. During a session, the practitioner will focus on specific areas of the body where they feel there may be blockages or imbalances in the energy flow. They will then use their hands to channel this energy into these areas to restore balance and harmony within the body.

Reiki therapy can be part of a holistic approach to recovery from narcissistic abuse. It helps victims reconnect with themselves deeper to begin healing from past trauma and reclaiming their power.

Transpersonal Therapy

Transpersonal therapy is a type of psychotherapy that integrates spiritual traditions and rituals into modern psychology. It focuses on the individual's whole being, including physical, emotional, intellectual, creative, and spiritual aspects. This approach to therapy emphasizes positive influences and role models to help individuals heal from trauma and increase their self-confidence. Transpersonal therapy is beneficial in narcissistic abuse recovery as it allows individuals to reconnect with themselves and find meaning in life beyond the abuse.

Through transpersonal therapy, individuals can gain insight into their behavior and learn how to cope with difficult emotions such as guilt, shame, or anger. They can also explore how their past experiences have shaped them and how they can use those experiences to create a better future. Additionally, transpersonal therapy helps individuals develop healthier relationships by learning how to set boundaries and communicate more effectively.

Transpersonal therapy allows individuals who have experienced narcissistic abuse to heal from their trauma.

Through this approach, individuals can gain insight into their behavior and learn how to create healthier relationships with others while also finding meaning in life beyond the abuse.

Art Therapy

Art therapy is a form of psychotherapy that uses creative activities such as drawing, painting, sculpting, and collaging to help people express their emotions and thoughts. It is often used in the recovery process from narcissistic abuse, as it can help individuals understand their feelings and experiences in a safe and supportive environment.

Through art therapy, individuals can explore difficult topics without verbalizing them. This allows them to express themselves in a way that feels comfortable for them. Art therapists are trained to recognize the underlying meanings behind the artwork and provide insight into how these symbols may be related to an individual's life experiences. They also offer guidance on how to use art-making as a tool for self-expression and healing.

In addition to providing emotional support, art therapy can also help individuals develop healthier coping skills. By engaging in creative activities, individuals can learn new ways of dealing with stress, anxiety, depression, and other issues related to narcissistic abuse recovery. Through this process of self-exploration and expression, they can gain insight into their needs and wants while developing more effective strategies for managing difficult emotions.

Art therapy is a valuable tool for those recovering from narcissistic abuse. It provides an opportunity for individuals to express themselves in a safe space while gaining insight into their own experiences and developing healthier coping skills.

Music Therapy

Music has been used for centuries to heal emotional pain and trauma. It is a powerful tool to help people process and heal from abuse. Music therapy is a type of therapy that uses music to help people express their feelings and work through difficult emotions.

Music helps us to access our emotions safely, allowing us to explore them without feeling overwhelmed or judged. It can provide an outlet for expression, enabling us to process our experiences and make sense of them. Music can also be used as a distraction from painful memories, providing comfort and relaxation during distress.

In music therapy, the therapist will use different types of music, such as singing, playing instruments, or listening to recordings, to facilitate healing. The therapist may also use songwriting as part of the therapeutic process, helping clients to express their feelings creatively. Through this process, clients can gain insight into their experiences and learn how to cope with difficult emotions.

The long-term benefits of music therapy are numerous. Studies have shown that regular music therapy sessions can reduce stress and anxiety levels, improve mood and self-expression, increase motivation, provide emotional release, and even help treat dementia. Music therapy has also been found to improve communication skills by assisting people to identify and name emotions in a safe setting. Additionally, it can help with physical discomfort by improving respiration, lowering blood pressure, increasing cardiac output, reducing heart rate variability, and improving overall physical health.

Music therapy is an effective way to promote both physical and mental health in the long term. Using music as a therapeutic tool to reduce stress and anxiety levels while providing emotional release and improved communication skills can be an invaluable resource for those looking to improve their overall well-being.

***

Deciding to get professional help for narcissistic abuse can be difficult. It's important to recognize that narcissistic abuse is a form of emotional and psychological abuse, and it can have serious long-term effects on your mental health.

Narcissistic abusers are self-aggrandizing and self-centered, and they manipulate others into giving them excessive attention by using words and actions. They lack empathy, making understanding how their behavior affects those around them difficult. As a result, they may not recognize or take responsibility for their abusive behavior.

The effects of narcissistic abuse can be devastating and long-lasting. Victims may experience low self-worth, depression, anxiety, post-traumatic stress disorder (PTSD), physical symptoms such as headaches or stomachaches, difficulty sleeping or concentrating, and more.

If you think you're in an abusive relationship with someone with a narcissistic personality disorder (NPD), seeking professional help as soon as possible is essential. A therapist can provide support and guidance as you work through the trauma associated with narcissistic abuse. They can also help you develop healthy coping skills to manage your emotions in the future.

It's also important to remember that you are not alone in this process. Many resources are available to help victims of narcissistic abuse find healing and recovery—from online support groups to hotlines dedicated to assisting in times of need.

No matter your situation, know there is hope for recovery from narcissistic abuse—and you don't have to go through it alone.

Chapter 9

Divorce and Family Court

S   hould I Stay or Should I Go

It can be challenging to decide to stay or leave a narcissistic relationship. Narcissists tend to make bad relationship partners, as they cannot feel empathy or offer real love. They may seem entitled, act superior to others, and not empathize with your needs. It is important to remember that you deserve better and build a support network with friends and family who will listen and provide emotional support.

If you decide to stay in the relationship, it is crucial to constantly remind yourself of your worth and set boundaries for how you will be treated. It would be best if you also strengthened your relationships with your empathetic friends to have an outlet for when things get tough.

On the other hand, if you decide that leaving the relationship is best for you, it is vital to be prepared for the narcissist's reaction. Narcissistic partners often keep misery going for their partners by trying to cut them down to build themselves up. Leaving a narcissistic relationship can be an incredibly difficult and emotionally draining experience.

Narcissists are known for their manipulative behavior, which often involves gaslighting, guilt-tripping, and other tactics to keep their partners in the relationship. When someone decides to leave a narcissistic relationship, they can expect a backlash from the narcissist.

The narcissist may attempt to make their partner feel guilty for leaving by blaming them for the breakup or trying to make them feel like they are abandoning them. They may also try to manipulate their partner into staying with them by making promises they do not intend to keep. Additionally, the narcissist may become angry and lash out at their partner to make them stay. This could involve verbal abuse, threats, or even physical violence.

It is important to remember that none of this behavior is acceptable and that it is never okay for someone to be treated this way. If you are in a narcissistic relationship and decide to leave, it is essential to have a plan to safely exit the situation without facing further backlash from the narcissist.

Regardless of your decision, it would be best to prioritize taking care of yourself first and foremost. Taking time for self-care activities such as exercising, meditating, journaling, or talking with a therapist can help clarify what is best for your mental health and well-being.

Creating An Exit Strategy

Leaving a narcissistic relationship can be difficult, but it is possible. Here are some tips to help you make the transition smooth and safe.

1. Prepare before you leave: Take the time to plan and prepare for your departure. Ensure you have a support system, such as friends or family, who can provide emotional support and practical help if needed. Consider setting up a safety plan that includes having an emergency contact, changing your locks, and having a place to stay if necessary.

2. Avoid unnecessary conversation: When leaving a narcissistic relationship, avoiding engaging in unnecessary conversations with your partner is essential. This will help prevent them from manipulating or controlling you during this vulnerable time.

3. Reduce contact: Once you've decided to leave the relationship, reduce contact with your partner as much as possible. This means no more phone calls or text messages, no social media interactions, and no physical contact.

4. Get ready for retaliation: Unfortunately, when leaving a narcissistic relationship, there is often some form of retaliation from the other person involved. Be prepared for this by having a safety plan and always staying alert.

5. Put away reminders of the relationship: It can be helpful to remove any reminders of the relationship from your home or workplace so that you don't have to constantly be reminded of it when you're trying to move on with your life.

6. Emotionally detach yourself: To fully heal from the trauma of being in a narcissistic relationship, it's important to emotionally detach yourself from the situation and focus on taking care of yourself first and foremost. This could include activities like taking bubble baths, journaling, getting massages, practicing meditation or yoga, making artwork, or spending time in nature - whatever helps you feel better about yourself and allows you to process what happened healthily without letting it consume your thoughts too much.

7. Block all methods of contact: Finally, make sure that once you've left the narcissist behind that they are blocked from all forms of communication - email, phone calls, WhatsApp messages, etc. - so that they cannot reach out in an attempt at manipulation or control over you again in future years down the line when they may think they have another chance with you again after some time has passed since leaving them behind initially. Creating a safety plan is a vital step to take if you are feeling suicidal or in crisis. A safety plan can help you identify warning signs of potential trouble and provide strategies to cope with difficult emotions.

Leaving an abusive relationship can also be a difficult and dangerous process. It is essential to have a safety plan in place before attempting to flee. Here are some tips for creating a safety plan:

1. Identify safe people and places you can go to if you need help. This could include friends, family members,

or organizations like the National Domestic Violence Hotline (https://www.thehotline.org/).

2. Ensure you have access to money and other resources that may be needed in an emergency. This could include having cash on hand or setting up a bank account in your name only that your partner needs to learn about.

3. Have important documents, such as birth certificates, social security cards, passports, etc., ready and accessible so you can take them with you if necessary.

4. Create an emergency bag with essential items such as clothes, medications, copies of important documents, and any other items that may be needed in case of an emergency evacuation from your home.

5. Consider changing your daily routine so that it is more unpredictable and harder for your abuser to track you down if they try to find you after leaving the relationship.

6. Make arrangements for temporary housing or shelter until more permanent living arrangements can be made after leaving the relationship.

7. Let trusted family members or friends know about the situation so they can support you and help keep you safe if necessary.

8.

Contact local law enforcement or domestic violence hotlines for additional help and advice on how to stay safe while leaving an abusive relationship (https://www.helpguide.org/articles/abuse/getting-out-of-an-abusive-relationship).

9. Warning signs a crisis may develop, such as thoughts, images, mood, situation, or behavior.

10. Coping strategies that can help manage difficult emotions, such as deep breathing exercises, journaling, or talking to someone you trust.

11. A support system of people who can provide emotional and practical support during a crisis. This could include family members, friends, or mental health professionals like therapists and counselors.

12. Professional agencies that can assist in times of need, such as the National Suicide Prevention Lifeline (1-800-273-8255) or Crisis Text Line (text HOME to 741741).

13. Ways to make your environment safer by removing any items that could be used for self-harm and avoiding triggers that could lead to a crisis.

A safety plan can help reduce the risk of future harm and provide guidance when facing abusive and difficult situations. Reviewing your safety plan regularly is essential, so it remains up-to-date and relevant to your current needs.

Document Document Document!

When divorcing a narcissist, it is crucial to document everything. This includes any communication between you and your spouse, court documents, and financial records related to the divorce. Documentation can be used as evidence in court if needed, and it will also help protect you from any false accusations or claims made by your spouse. In addition to the standard documents required for any divorce case, some specific documents can help when divorcing a narcissist. For example, logs of interactions between you and your spouse can provide evidence of their behavior or lack thereof. Photographs of assets or other important items can also help prove ownership or possession of certain items. Finally, having copies of any court orders issued during the divorce proceedings will ensure that both parties abide by the terms set forth by the court.

There are several ways to document narcissistic abuse. Keeping a journal is one of the most effective ways to record your experiences. Writing down details such as dates, times, and events can help you remember what happened and provide evidence if needed. You can also keep track of emails, text messages, or other forms of communication that contain abusive language or threats. Taking screenshots of social media posts or conversations can also help document abuse.

Documenting physical signs of abuse, such as bruises or cuts. Take photos or videos of these injuries and save them for future reference. If possible, seek medical attention for any physical injuries and keep copies of medical records or reports related to the abuse.

Finally, talking about your experiences with trusted friends and family members who can provide emotional support and help validate your story is essential. They may also be able to provide additional information about the abuser's behavior that could be useful in documenting the abuse.

Documenting narcissistic abuse is an essential part of the healing process after a relationship with someone with NPD. Keeping detailed records will not only help you process your experience but could also be used as evidence if needed in the future.

Having all this information on hand can make filing for divorce much easier and less stressful. By keeping detailed records throughout the process, you can ensure that your rights are protected and that you have all the necessary information when it comes time to negotiate a settlement or go to court.

Finding The Right Divorce Lawyer

When divorcing a narcissist, it is vital to choose the right lawyer. A lawyer who understands Narcissistic Personality Disorder (NPD) can provide firm parenting plans and court orders without room for manipulation or wiggle room.

When selecting an attorney, it is essential to ask questions such as: how much experience do they have in dealing with complex family law cases concerning emotional/domestic abuse, high-conflict individuals, or contested child custody? It is also beneficial to look for an attorney who has handled many divorces and can provide tactical approaches to disarm the narcissist.

Here are some questions to ask family law attorneys when considering a divorce from a narcissist:

1. What is your definition of a "High Conflict" divorce?

2. Have you encountered opposing spouses who are narcissists before?

3. What strategies do you use when dealing with complex family law cases?

4. How much will my divorce cost?

5. Are you familiar with the tactics that narcissists use in divorce proceedings?

6. What advice do you have for someone divorcing a narcissist?

7. How can I protect myself and my assets during this process?

8. Do you understand how to deal with an NPD respondent (Narcissistic Personality Disorder)?

9. Are you experienced in child custody cases involving narcissistic parents?

10. What methods do you use to work effectively with clients divorcing a narcissist?

In addition, it is important to work closely with your lawyer and rely on their judgment and experience as your case proceeds. Your lawyer should be confident in their knowledge of the system and have an understanding of the judges, lawyers, and laws involved in your case.

Divorcing a narcissist can be complicated, but having a knowledgeable attorney on your side can help protect you and your assets throughout the process.

Avoid Using the Term Narcissism in Court

If your spouse or partner has not been formally diagnosed with NPD or narcissistic personality disorder, avoiding using the word "narcissism" in divorce court is essential. This can trigger the narcissist's rage and lead to further conflict. Judges, lawyers, and courts typically do not like hearing this term, as it can be overused in divorce and family court proceedings. Instead, it is best to focus on describing behaviors and characteristics associated with narcissistic behavior.

Common characteristics of narcissists include a need for control, lack of empathy, grandiosity, manipulation, and a tendency to blame others for their mistakes or shortcomings. Narcissists also tend to employ the same general tactics in divorce proceedings, such as trying to win at all costs and becoming obsessed with getting what they want from the divorce settlement.

Prepare yourself mentally, physically, and financially when divorcing a narcissist. Have a clear understanding of your rights and responsibilities under the law and access to legal advice if needed. It is also essential to remain calm and collected throughout the process to keep the situation from escalating into further conflict or chaos.

By being aware of these behaviors and characteristics associated with narcissistic behavior, you can better prepare yourself for potential conflicts during your divorce proceedings. By avoiding using the word "narcissism" in court and instead focusing on describing behaviors and characteristics associated with narcissistic behavior, you can help ensure that your divorce proceedings remain civil while protecting your interests.

Common Tactics Narcissists Use In Divorce Proceedings

Gaslighting is a common tactic used by narcissists in divorce proceedings. It involves manipulating someone into doubting their sanity or memory by denying facts or events that have occurred. This can be especially damaging in a legal context, leading to confusion and mistrust of the court system.

Narcissists may also refuse to cooperate with you and your legal team during the divorce proceedings. They may not provide necessary financial records or other documents for the case. This can make it difficult for you to get a fair settlement from the court.

Narcissists often use false accusations of abuse to discredit and intimidate their ex-partner, making it difficult for them to fight for custody or visitation rights. This type of abuse can be particularly damaging because it affects the victim emotionally and financially, as they may have to pay for legal fees and other costs associated with defending themselves against false accusations.

To protect yourself from narcissistic abuse during a divorce, it is essential to document all interactions with your former partner and keep copies of any relevant documents. It is also necessary to seek support from friends, family, or professionals who can provide emotional support and help you navigate the legal process. Additionally, if you are facing false accusations of abuse, remain calm and collected when responding to them so that you can present your case most effectively.

Narcissists often use the legal system to abuse their former partner during divorce proceedings financially. They may do this by filing frivolous lawsuits or dragging out court proceedings to gain an advantage. Additionally, they may attempt to manipulate the court system to maintain control over their former partner and draw out disputes as long as possible.

When divorcing a narcissist, be prepared and understand how they may attempt to use the legal system against them. Have an experienced family law attorney who can help protect you from such tactics. Your attorney should be prepared to explain narcissistic behavior and its effects on the court proceedings and provide strategies for dealing with it effectively. Additionally, your attorney should be familiar with techniques that narcissists use to exploit the legal system and be able to counter them accordingly.

Finally, if you are facing narcissistic abuse during a divorce, remember that you are not alone and that resources are available to help you through this difficult time. With the right support system, you can successfully navigate the legal process while protecting yourself from further harm.

Finally, narcissists often prolong conflict during divorce by refusing to settle and using provocative behavior to maintain control over the situation. This can include dragging out the process for as long as possible, blaming their spouse for marital problems, and resisting counseling. Narcissists may also react to the knowledge of a potential divorce with domestic violence or child abuse.

Be aware of these tactics when divorcing a narcissist so that you can prepare yourself for any potential challenges that may arise during the process. Be prepared mentally, physically, and financially when divorcing a narcissist to protect yourself from toxic behaviors. With proper preparation and understanding of these tactics, you will be better equipped to handle any issues during your divorce proceedings.

Stay Calm Through Divorce

As you go through divorce proceedings, it is essential to remain calm and not react to a narcissist, especially in court. Reacting to a narcissist can be detrimental, as it can lead to the narcissist using your reaction against you and manipulating the situation. Narcissists are adept at using people's emotions and responses to their advantage. If you stay calm, you can maintain control of the situation and protect yourself from being manipulated. It is also important to remember that any reaction you have will likely be used against you in court, so it is best to remain composed and collected.

Here are some tips for staying calm while in divorce court
with a narcissist:

1. Remain composed and collected. Don't let the
   narcissist get under your skin during the proceedings;
   try not to lose your temper or become emotional.

2. Work with a therapist to learn emotional regulation
   skills and techniques.

3. Set clear boundaries and stick to them. Ensure you
   know what acceptable behavior from both parties is,
   and don't allow violations of those boundaries.

4. Communicate effectively. Resist the urge to debate or
   defend yourself in court, as this will only fuel the
   narcissist's fire. Instead, focus on communicating
   clearly and calmly about the facts of the case.

5. Seek support from friends and family members who
   understand what you're going through and can provide
   emotional support during this difficult time.

6. Find something new that will take your mind off
   everything, such as a hobby or activity you enjoy doing
   outside of court proceedings.

7. Have realistic expectations about the outcome of the
   divorce proceedings; don't expect perfection or
   complete satisfaction with every decision made in
   court, as this is rarely achievable when divorcing a
   narcissistic spouse.

8. Prepare yourself mentally, physically, and financially for the divorce process; having a plan can help reduce stress levels during court proceedings.

9. Remember that you have rights, too; don't be afraid to assert them if necessary to protect yourself from any potential abuse or manipulation from your ex-spouse during divorce proceedings.

By following these tips, you can stay calm while in divorce court with a narcissist and ensure that you can make the best decisions for both parties without getting overwhelmed by their tactics or losing control of your emotions.

Set Realistic Expectations for Court

When divorcing a narcissist, family court is not a justice system but a legal one. Do not go into family court expecting justice. Family court is designed to resolve disputes between family members efficiently and cost-effectively. It does not provide the same level of protection as a criminal justice system, such as the right to a jury trial or appeal.

In family court, decisions are made based on the evidence presented by both parties and the applicable laws. The judge will consider all relevant factors, including any history of abuse or neglect by either party. The goal of the family court is to reach an agreement that is fair for both parties and protects the interests of any children involved.

Setting realistic expectations and assembling your support team is essential when divorcing a narcissist. Consider therapy for yourself and your children and document everything. Additionally, setting boundaries for yourself and understanding the impact of the narcissist on the divorce process are critical steps in navigating this situation.

Narcissists tend to lack a realistic sense of guilt or remorse, which makes it difficult for a divorce to be amicable without a sol third-party perspective. It is understood that the ultimate goal of a narcissist in divorce is to be proven right, and they will do whatever it takes to make that happen.

Regarding family court and custody cases, it is also essential to have realistic expectations. A judge or even negotiating couple rarely ends up with an exact split of assets from the marriage. In addition, when fighting for custody, set realistic expectations, as there is rarely a clear winner in these cases.

To understand co-parenting basics and the other parent's rights while focusing on the child's best interests. Retaining a capable custody lawyer can help you manage your expectations and prepare you for what lies ahead.

When preparing for divorce, it is helpful to ask for referrals from friends or look up local family law firms and ask if they can provide references you can talk to. Additionally, setting realistic expectations about how long the process will take can help put you on the road to recovery and a happier future.

It is also important to note that spouses of narcissists often seek individual therapy for help with feelings of loneliness, anxiety, and depression brought on by years of narcissistic abuse.

Overall, divorcing a narcissist requires patience and preparation to navigate this personality type's complex and skewed thinking. With proper guidance from mental health professionals and legal advisors, you can win your divorce from a narcissist.

What Is a TPO and When Can It Be Used

Filing for divorce can trigger what is called narcissistic rage in many narcissists. Narcissistic rage is an intense reaction to a perceived threat or injury to a person's self-esteem. It can manifest in different ways, from verbal outbursts and physical aggression to passive aggression and withdrawal. People with narcissistic personality disorder are particularly prone to this type of behavior. If you fear for your or your children's safety, you can file a TPO.

A Temporary Protection Order (TPO) is a court order issued by a judge that protects from harm or harassment for an individual. It can be requested by the person who needs protection, or someone on their behalf can order it. The TPO will typically include provisions such as prohibiting contact with the protected person, staying away from their home and workplace, and surrendering any firearms. Reasons to file a TPO include domestic violence, stalking, harassment, and threats of violence.

To qualify for a TPO (check your state requirements or consult your attorney), the petitioner must show that they have been the victim of family violence, sexual assault, stalking, or trafficking. The petitioner must also provide evidence that they are in immediate and present danger of further abuse if the TPO is not granted.

Once the petition has been filed with the court, a hearing will be scheduled so that both parties can present their case before a judge. If the judge finds sufficient evidence to grant the TPO, it will be issued and remain in effect until it expires or is modified by the court.

It's important to note that filing for a TPO does not guarantee protection from abuse or harassment; however, it may help provide peace of mind and safety for those who feel threatened by another person. If you believe you qualify for a TPO, it's vital to seek legal advice as soon as possible.

Guardian Ad Litems

A guardian ad litem (GAL) is an individual appointed by the court to represent the best interests of a child when parents cannot agree on allocating parental rights and responsibilities. The GAL is tasked with investigating the case and recommending to the court what would be in the child's best interest regarding custody. The GAL advocates for those who cannot advocate for themselves in court proceedings, such as children and adults with mental incapacity or disability.

The GAL's primary function is to investigate the case and provide recommendations to the court about what would be in the best interest of the child or adult they represent. This may involve conducting interviews with parents and other individuals involved in the child's life, reviewing school or medical records, or gathering social service reports. Once their investigation is complete, the GAL will present their findings and recommendations to the court.

Regarding divorce court proceedings, a guardian ad litem (GAL) may be appointed by the family court at the request of one of the parties involved. A GAL is a legally appointed attorney assigned by a judge in child custody cases. The GAL will meet with each parent individually and ask questions that are not on the questionnaire.

Whether to request a Guardian ad Litem (GAL) can be a significant strategic move for a parent involved in a child custody battle. Generally, GALs are appointed when a person engaged in a legal case cannot adequately represent themselves due to being a minor or having special needs. In some states, GALs may be required if certain circumstances arise during the proceedings.

Parents can request the appointment of a guardian ad litem if the case circumstances don't already require it. If an appointment is not needed, it's up to the judge's discretion as to whether or not they appoint one. It's also important to note that unless otherwise ordered by the court, the requesting party shall bear all costs associated with appointing and compensating the GAL.

A Guardian ad Litem (GAL) may be required by law when the welfare of a child is a matter of concern for the court. GALs advocate for children and serve as a voice in legal proceedings to ensure their best interests are represented. In some cases, GALs may be appointed to investigate allegations of abuse or neglect, claims of parental alienation, provide recommendations on custody arrangements, or represent the child's wishes in court. They also work with other professionals, such as social workers and psychologists, to meet the child's needs.

In summary, when deciding whether or not to request a Guardian Ad Litem in your divorce court situation, you should consider all factors involved and consult with an experienced family law attorney who can help you make an informed decision about what's best for your particular situation.

***

Divorcing a narcissist can be a difficult and emotionally draining experience. Be prepared mentally, physically, and financially before beginning the process. There are two ways to get a divorce: settlement or trial; however, many narcissists refuse to settle. During a divorce, limit communication with your ex-spouse and keep copies of all documents. Additionally, having a strong lawyer and therapist can help you navigate the process and protect your rights. Build your support tribe with friends and family to support you. It is also important to remember that even if your ex agreed to part ways, they might not be keen on "losing" in court. The best thing you can do is minimize contact with them and avoid any potential conflict.

Chapter 10

Co-Parenting With A Narcissist

C o-parenting is a post-divorce arrangement in which parents participate jointly in their children's upbringing and care. It involves working together to provide the best possible environment for the child, regardless of any differences between the two parents. This includes making decisions about education, health care, and other aspects of the child's life. Co-parenting also requires parents to communicate openly and honestly with each other and their children.

In co-parenting, a child is free to visit family without hesitation. Living in nearby locations gives a better chance to provide this privilege to a child. Both parents need to put their own emotions aside and focus on what is best for their children. Successful co-parenting means your emotions must take a back seat to your children's needs—anger, resentment, or hurt.

Healthy co-parenting involves two parents who are no longer together raising their child (or children) jointly to ensure they have a safe and secure environment in which to grow up.

Some signs of healthy co-parenting include prioritizing direct communication between the two parents, keeping adult responsibilities between them, avoiding forcing children to choose sides, using a positive tone when talking about the other parent, and controlling emotions during interactions. Both parents need to make sure that their feelings do not interfere with their ability to provide a stable home life for their children.

Creating boundaries is also essential in successful co-parenting. Parents should establish clear rules and expectations for both themselves and their children to prevent conflict from arising. This includes setting limits on discussing topics between the two households and establishing guidelines for handling disagreements. Additionally, both parents must remain consistent with discipline, so the child feels understood and supported by different parenting styles.

Emotions are a part of life, but it's important to put them aside and focus on the child's needs when it comes to parenting. Emotions can cloud our judgment and lead us to make decisions that may not be in the best interest of our children. It's essential to step back and consider what is best for the child before making any decisions.

When emotions are involved, thinking clearly and objectively about a situation can be challenging. We may react impulsively or decide based on our feelings rather than what is best for the child. This can lead to poor decision-making that could have long-term consequences for our children.

It's essential to remember that parenting is not just about providing love and support; it also involves making tough decisions that may not always be popular with our children. By taking a step back and focusing on what is best for them, we can ensure that we are making sound decisions that will benefit them in the long run.

Putting emotions aside and focusing on the child's needs is essential to provide them with the best care and guidance. It takes practice, but pausing before responding or acting can ensure you are doing what is best for your children.

Remember that it's best to keep a positive tone when talking about the other parent. This will help your children feel secure and comfortable with both parents. Even if you and the other parent are not on good terms, try to focus on the positive qualities they possess. This can be challenging sometimes, but it will benefit your children in the long run.

When discussing their other parent, emphasize their positive qualities such as kindness, intelligence, or humor. Let them know that you approve of their other parent and that they have a special relationship with them. Avoid making negative comments or engaging in arguments in front of your child. Instead, focus on keeping conversations calm and productive.

It's also important to avoid using your child as a messenger between you and the other parent. If there is something you need to communicate with them, do so directly rather than through your child. This will help protect them from feeling caught in the middle of any disagreements between you two.

Keeping a positive tone when talking about the other parent can help create an environment where your children feel secure and comfortable with both parents.

One of the essential rules when co-parenting is to never use your child as a messenger between you and your ex. Doing so can put an unnecessary burden on your child, leading to feelings of guilt or confusion.

Communicate directly with the other parent whenever possible. If you need to pass along a message, ensure it is done in person or over the phone instead of through your child. This will help keep them out of the middle and allow them to focus on being kids.

If you are tempted to use your child as a messenger, take a step back and consider how it might affect them. It's better for everyone involved if you take responsibility for communicating with your ex instead of putting that burden on your child.

Communication Rules for Co-Parenting

1. Use respectful language when communicating with one another.

2. Keep communication brief, to the point, and always about the kids.

Discuss important decisions together.

4. Help children feel secure by maintaining consistency in parenting styles and rules.

5. Refrain from disrespecting each other or using passive aggressiveness, sarcasm, cuss words, or anything else that isn't polite and appropriate.

6. Communicate in a business-like manner without name-calling or any other harmful behavior.

7. Follow the parenting plan and custody schedule established by both parties.

8. Ignore a toxic, narcissistic, or high-conflict ex to benefit the children involved in co-parenting arrangements.

Maintaining Consistency In Both Households

Parenting styles and rules can be challenging when children are in two different households. This is especially true if the households have different parenting styles and rules. Communicate with both households about expectations, values, and discipline techniques to ensure consistency. Parents should also work together to create a unified plan for handling common issues such as bedtime, screen time, and homework. Additionally, parents should strive to provide consistent rewards and consequences for their children's behavior.

It is also helpful for parents to discuss any changes in parenting styles or rules with each other before making them. This will help ensure that both households are on the same page and that changes are implemented consistently across both homes. Finally, consistency does not mean rigidity; flexibility is key in parenting styles and rules.

Regarding parenting styles and rules, consistency does not mean rigidity. Parenting styles can be divided into four main categories: authoritarian, authoritative, permissive, and uninvolved. Authoritarian parenting is demanding but not responsive, while permissive parenting is responsive but not demanding. Authoritative parenting balances responsiveness and firmness, while neglectful or uninvolved parenting involves little to no interaction with the child.

Authoritative parenting is often seen as the most effective parenting style, as it provides structure and guidance for children without being overly strict or rigid. This parenting style allows for flexibility in rules and expectations while maintaining consistency in discipline and expectations. It also encourages open communication between parent and child so that both parties can work together to find beneficial solutions for everyone involved.

Ultimately, consistency does not mean rigidity regarding parenting styles and rules. Flexibility in rules allows parents to adjust their approach based on each child's individual needs while still providing a sense of security through consistent discipline and expectations.

By following these tips, parents can help maintain consistency in parenting styles and household rules.

Parallel Parenting

Co-parenting with a narcissist can be a challenging experience, making co-parenting difficult to collaborate on parenting decisions, as the narcissist may not consider the needs of the other parent or their children.

Narcissists often have difficulty accepting responsibility for their actions and may attempt to shift blame onto others. This can create tension and mistrust, making it challenging to work together productively. In addition, narcissists may use manipulative tactics such as guilt-tripping or gaslighting to get what they want from the other parent.

It is important to remember that co-parenting with a narcissist does not have to be impossible. Setting clear boundaries and expectations can help ensure that both parents are respected and that decisions are made in the children's best interests. It is also essential to maintain open communication so that any issues can be discussed respectfully. Finally, seeking professional help from a therapist or mediator can provide additional support when navigating this challenging situation and using parallel parenting if the conflict is too intense.

Parallel parenting is a type of co-parenting in which each parent has their parenting style when the children are with them. It is an arrangement in which parents who are now divorced or separated can co-parent by disengaging from each other and instituting their parenting methods. Parallel parenting allows the parents to spend time with and care for their children independently, without traditional co-parenting and communication. It involves detailed parenting plans that clearly outline pick-up times, locations, and schedules and refrain from frequent contact with one another.

Parallel parenting may be necessary when one parent is narcissistic. This type of parenting involves each parent taking responsibility for their own decisions and actions while maintaining communication and cooperation with the other parent. It allows both parents to have a say in their child's upbringing without having to interact directly with each other. This can benefit children of narcissistic parents by enabling them to have two loving and supportive parents who are not in conflict with each other. Parallel parenting also allows children to develop relationships with both parents without fear of being caught in the middle of any arguments or power struggles between them.

A parallel parenting plan of communication is a plan that allows parents to communicate with each other while minimizing contact. It is designed to ensure that both parents can spend adequate time with their children and have the necessary information to make decisions about their care.

The first step in creating a parallel parenting communication plan is determining how you will split time with the kids. This should include details such as pick-up times, locations, and schedules. The next step is to decide on the start and end times for each parent's time with the child. Ensure these times are communicated between parents to avoid confusion or overlap in parenting responsibilities.

It is also vital for both parents to agree on how they will communicate with each other regarding their child's care. This could include setting up regular check-ins via phone or email or using an online platform such as Google Docs or Dropbox, where both parents can access important documents related to their child's care. Additionally, it is beneficial for both parents to agree on a method of communication for resolving any disputes that arise during co-parenting.

Finally, Parents must understand and respect each other's parenting styles when communicating about their child's care. This means being open and honest about your expectations and knowledge that your co-parent may have different ideas about what works best for your child. By respecting each other's parenting styles, you can create a more harmonious relationship between you and your co-parent, ultimately benefiting your child in the long run.

Creating a parallel parenting plan of communication can help ensure that both parents can provide adequate care for their children while minimizing contact between them. By following these steps, you can create a plan that works best for everyone involved to ensure the well-being of your children during this difficult time.

Use of Co-Parenting Apps

Co-parenting apps are digital tools that help separated parents manage their shared parenting responsibilities. These apps provide a secure platform for communication, scheduling, and document sharing between co-parents.

The primary benefit of using a co-parenting app is that it can help reduce conflict between parents by providing a central place to store important information and communicate organizationally. Co-parenting apps also allow parents to keep track of important dates, such as doctor's appointments and school events, and share documents like medical records or court orders. Additionally, many co-parenting apps offer features such as expense tracking and payment reminders which can be especially helpful when managing child support payments.

Co-parenting apps can also be a great tool to help reduce conflict between parents. These apps provide an efficient and secure way for parents to communicate, share information, and manage their parenting responsibilities. With features such as shared calendars, messaging, expense tracking, and document storage, co-parenting apps make it easy for parents to stay organized and on the same page. This helps reduce misunderstandings and disagreements that can lead to conflict. Additionally, many co-parenting apps offer built-in tools such as mediation services or dispute resolution systems that allow parents to resolve conflicts without going through the court system. Co-parenting apps can help reduce stress and conflict between parents by providing a safe space for communication and collaboration.

Several apps are now available to help divorced parents manage their co-parenting responsibilities. Here are the top 5 co-parenting apps that can help make life easier for both parents and children.

1. Our Family Wizard: This app is designed to keep communication between divorced parents organized

and efficient. It allows parents to quickly exchange messages, share calendars, track expenses, and more.

2. Coparently: This app helps divorced parents stay organized by providing them with a shared calendar, task list, expense tracking, and other features that make it easy to manage parenting responsibilities.

3. Cozi: This app is designed to help families stay connected and organized by providing a shared calendar and task list that can be accessed from anywhere. It also includes grocery lists and meal planning tools, making managing family life easier for everyone involved.

4. 2Houses: This app is designed explicitly for divorced or separated couples who need help efficiently managing their parenting responsibilities. It provides features such as shared calendars, expense tracking, document sharing, messaging tools, and more.

5. Google Calendar: While not explicitly designed for co-parenting purposes, Google Calendar is still an excellent tool for keeping track of appointments and important dates related to parenting responsibilities. It's free and easy to use on any device or computer with an internet connection.

Co-parenting apps can be a valuable tool for helping separated parents stay organized and on the same page regarding parenting responsibilities. By providing an easy way to communicate and share information, these apps can make co-parenting much smoother and less stressful for both parties involved.

Healthy co-parenting is beneficial for children in many ways. It allows both parents to remain involved in their children's lives, creating a solid bond. Co-parenting also helps children maintain loving relationships with both parents and provides them with stability and consistency in expectations, communication, and schedules from both parents. Additionally, it helps lower the stress and anxiety levels of the children as well as reduce conflicts between the two households. Ultimately, healthy co-parenting creates a safe environment for children to thrive in and gives them a sense of security and self-worth.

Chapter 11

Healing and Rebuilding Your Life

Healing from a narcissistic relationship can be a long and challenging process. Understand the stages of healing to make progress toward recovery.

The first stage is recognizing that you have been in a narcissistic relationship. This involves acknowledging the signs of abuse, such as manipulation, gaslighting, and emotional invalidation. Once you have identified that you have been in an abusive relationship, building a support system of people who can provide emotional support and understanding is essential.

The second stage is learning how to set boundaries with yourself and others. This includes setting limits on what you will tolerate from others and learning how to say no when necessary. It also involves learning how to take care of yourself emotionally and physically by engaging in self-care activities such as journaling, exercise, meditation, or talking to a therapist.

The third stage is rebuilding your sense of self-worth and confidence. This may involve challenging negative beliefs about yourself that were reinforced during the narcissistic relationship. It also involves focusing on your strengths and accomplishments rather than dwelling on past mistakes or failures.

The fourth stage is forgiving yourself for staying in the narcissistic relationship for so long and forgiving the other person for their behavior. This step is essential for moving forward without being weighed down by guilt or resentment towards yourself or the other person involved in the relationship.

It is important to remember that closure does not need to come from the narcissist; instead, it must come from within yourself. Allow yourself time and space to grieve and heal at your own pace, and know that you will eventually reach a place of peace and acceptance.

Finally, remember that healing from a narcissistic relationship takes time and patience but can be done with effort and dedication. Take things one day at a time and focus on caring for yourself mentally and physically throughout this process.

Grief

After a relationship with a narcissist, it can be challenging to find acceptance. Acknowledge the harm that was done and mourn the ending of the relationship. This healing process from narcissistic abuse includes accepting that closure cannot come from the narcissist but must come from within.

The stages of grief when realizing a narcissistic relationship are similar to those defined by Elisabeth Kubler Ross: denial, anger, bargaining, depression, and acceptance.

Denial is the first stage of grief and involves refusing to accept the reality of the situation. It can be challenging to accept that your relationship has ended, and it is normal to feel disbelief or shock.

The second stage is anger. This can manifest in many ways, such as feeling angry at yourself for staying in the relationship for so long or at your partner for their behavior. It is essential to recognize and express these feelings healthily, such as by talking to a friend or writing down your thoughts.

The third stage is bargaining. This involves trying to negotiate with yourself or your partner to undo what has happened or change the situation's outcome. You may wish that things had been different or that you could have done something differently.

The fourth stage is depression which can involve feeling overwhelmed by sadness and hopelessness about the future without your partner. It can also include feeling guilty about leaving the relationship and struggling with low self-esteem due to being in an unhealthy relationship for so long.

The fifth and final stage is acceptance which involves coming to terms with what has happened and realizing there was nothing you could have done differently. Acceptance does not mean that you are happy about what has happened but instead that you can move forward without being weighed down by guilt or regret about what has happened in the past.

Leaving a narcissistic relationship can be an emotionally challenging process but understanding these stages of grief can help you navigate this difficult time more effectively and ultimately move forward with your life in a healthier way. It is essential to go through these stages to heal. Taking time for yourself and getting rest can help with this process.

It is also important to reconnect with anyone you may have been isolated from while in an abusive relationship with a narcissist. Reaching out for support can help you on your journey toward finding acceptance after a narcissistic relationship.

Identifying Co-Dependency

Co-dependency is a behavioral pattern often manifested in individuals struggling to maintain healthy relationships. Co-dependent people typically have low self-esteem, a strong desire for approval and validation from others, and a fear of rejection or abandonment. They may also tend to prioritize the needs and desires of others over their own, leading to a lack of self-care and self-worth.

Co-dependent individuals are often drawn to the narcissist's charisma, confidence, and charm in narcissistic relationships. However, the narcissist's need for control and attention can be overwhelming, and the co-dependent person may feel responsible for meeting the narcissist's needs at their own expense.

Common characteristics of co-dependent individuals include:

1. Low self-esteem: Co-dependent individuals often struggle with inadequacy and may seek validation from others to feel better about themselves.

2. Difficulty setting boundaries: Co-dependent individuals may have difficulty saying no or setting boundaries with others, leading to a lack of personal space and boundaries.

3. Fear of rejection or abandonment: Co-dependent individuals may have an intense fear of rejection or abandonment, leading them to cling to relationships even when unhealthy.

4. People-pleasing tendencies: Co-dependent individuals often prioritize the needs and desires of others over their own, leading to a lack of self-care and self-worth.

5. Difficulty making decisions: Co-dependent individuals may struggle with decision-making, often relying on the opinions of others to guide their choices.

Healing from co-dependency is a process that can take time and effort, but it is possible with patience and perseverance. Here are some steps that can help:

1. Educate yourself: Learning about co-dependency and how it manifests in your life is an essential first step in

healing. Many resources are available, including books, support groups, and therapy.

2. Set boundaries: Co-dependent individuals often struggle with setting boundaries, but it's crucial for their healing. Start by identifying your needs and communicating them to others. Learn to say no to requests that don't align with your needs and take time for yourself when needed.

3. Practice self-care: Co-dependent individuals often prioritize the needs of others over their own. Learning to prioritize self-care is essential for healing. Take time to do things that bring you joy and fulfillment, such as hobbies, exercise, or spending time with friends and family.

4. Build self-esteem: Low self-esteem is a common characteristic of co-dependent individuals. To build self-esteem, focus on your strengths and accomplishments. Practice self-compassion, and challenge negative self-talk.

5. Seek support: Healing from co-dependency can be challenging; asking for help is okay. Consider joining a support group or working with a therapist specializing in co-dependency.

6. Develop healthy relationships: Healthy relationships are essential for healing from co-dependency. Seek relationships with people who respect your boundaries and encourage your growth.

7. Practice forgiveness: Co-dependency often stems from past traumas and hurts. Learning to forgive yourself and others is crucial for healing.

Remember that healing from co-dependency is a journey, not a destination. It takes time and effort, but it is possible to break free from unhealthy behavior patterns and build a healthy, fulfilling life with patience and perseverance.

Breaking The Trauma Bond

Trauma bonding is an unhealthy attachment that can form between two people in a relationship where one person is being abused. It occurs when the abuser uses a cycle of abuse, devaluation, and positive reinforcement to manipulate the victim into forming an emotional connection with them. This bond can be challenging to break because it is based on fear and manipulation rather than genuine love or respect.

The cycle of abuse typically starts with the abuser using physical, emotional, or sexual violence against their victim. This creates feelings of fear and helplessness in the victim, which can lead them to become dependent on their abuser for protection and validation. The abuser then follows up this violence with periods of kindness or affection, which can make the victim feel grateful for any positive attention they receive from their abuser. This creates loyalty towards their abuser, even though they are still being mistreated.

The trauma bond created by this cycle of abuse can be powerful and hard to break because it relies on fear and manipulation rather than genuine love or respect. Victims may find themselves unable to leave their abusers despite knowing that they are being mistreated because they have developed an emotional attachment to them. To break this bond, victims must first recognize that it exists and understand how it was created to begin taking steps toward healing from the trauma they have experienced.

Breaking a trauma bond requires time, effort, and support from friends and family members who can provide emotional support during this challenging process. It also involves developing healthier coping mechanisms, such as self-care activities like journaling or meditation, that help victims control their emotions instead of relying on their abuser for validation or comfort. With patience and dedication, victims can eventually break free from these unhealthy attachments and build healthier relationships with themselves and others.

Breaking the trauma bond with a narcissist can be difficult and painful. It is important to remember that you are not alone in this journey and that help is available.

The first step in breaking the trauma bond is recognizing it for what it is. Trauma bonding occurs when an abuser provides intermittent rewards and punishments, creating a psychological connection between the abuser and the abused. This connection can make it difficult for abuse survivors to leave their abusers, as they feel emotionally connected and even loyal to them.

The next step in breaking the trauma bond is to understand why it exists. Narcissists use this type of bonding to control their victims by providing them with intermittent rewards and punishments that keep them hooked on their abuser's attention. This cycle of abuse creates an unhealthy dependency on the narcissist, making it hard for victims to break free from their grasp.

Finally, finding support to break the trauma bond with a narcissist is vital. Seeking professional help from a therapist or counselor can be beneficial in understanding your situation better and developing strategies for coping with the emotional pain associated with leaving an abusive relationship. Additionally, joining support groups or online forums can provide valuable insight into how other people have broken free from similar situations and offer encouragement throughout your recovery process.

Here are some tips to help you break the cycle:

1. Educate yourself about trauma bonds and the dynamics of unhealthy relationships.

2. Focus on the present moment and practice mindfulness to stay grounded in reality.

3. Create space between you and your abuser by setting boundaries and avoiding contact with them as much as possible.

4. Seek support from friends, family, or a therapist who can help you.

5. Practice self-care and take time for yourself to focus on healing and rebuilding your life without toxic relationships.

6. Make plans for the future to help you move forward in a positive direction away from your abuser.

7. Challenge any negative thoughts or beliefs about yourself instilled by your abuser, such as self-blame or guilt for what happened in the relationship.

8. Ask yourself questions that will help you gain perspective on the situation, such as "What would I tell someone else in my situation?" or "What do I need right now?"

9. Shift your focus away from the abuser and towards activities that bring you joy, such as hobbies or spending time with people who make you feel safe and supported.

10. Take one step at a time; breaking free of a trauma bond does not happen overnight but takes time, patience, and effort to heal fully.

Breaking the trauma bond with a narcissist requires strength, courage, and resilience, but taking the proper steps toward healing is possible.

Forgiveness

Forgiving yourself and the other person involved in a narcissistic relationship can be difficult, but it is possible, and it may take time as you begin your healing journey. Here are some steps to help you on your journey of self-forgiveness and reconciliation:

1. Acknowledge your feelings - Taking the time to recognize and accept all of your emotions surrounding the situation is essential. This includes any anger, hurt, sadness, or guilt you may feel.

2. Reframe the situation - After acknowledging your feelings, look at the problem differently. Consider how the relationship affected both parties and why it ended up as it did.

3. Practice self-compassion - Remember to be kind to yourself and that everyone makes mistakes sometimes. It's essential to forgive yourself for any wrongs committed during the relationship to move forward with a clear conscience.

4. Take responsibility for your actions - Acknowledge your role in the relationship and take ownership. This will help you understand why things happened as they did and will allow you to move forward with more clarity and understanding.

5. Reach out for support - If needed, seek professional help or support from friends or family members who can provide an outside perspective on the situation and offer guidance on moving forward healthily.

6. Reconcile with the other person - Reach out to the person involved to reconcile and find closure on what happened between you both during the relationship. This could include an honest conversation about what

went wrong or simply apologizing for any hurt caused by either party during the relationship.

Reconnecting With Friends and Family

If you've been in a narcissistic relationship, it can be difficult to reconnect with old friends and family you lost contact with due to the isolation you may have experienced. You may feel like you have changed and no longer fit in with the same people or activities that once brought you joy. It is important to remember that your old friends still care about you and want to support you during this time. Here are some tips for reconnecting with old friends after a narcissistic relationship:

1. Reach out and let them know what has been going on in your life. It's essential, to be honest about how the experience has affected you, but also try to focus on the positive aspects of your life now.

2. Ask them how they've been doing and take an interest in their lives. This will help build trust and create a sense of connection between the two of you again.

3. Suggest meeting up for coffee or lunch to catch up in person. This will allow you to talk openly without distractions or interruptions from other people or technology.

4. Make plans for future activities such as going out for dinner, attending a concert, or even just getting together for drinks at home. Having something fun and

exciting planned will make it easier for both of you to look forward to spending time together again!

5. Don't forget to thank them for being there for you during this difficult time – it means more than they know!

Reconnecting with old friends after a narcissistic relationship can feel scary, but it doesn't have to be overwhelming! With patience and understanding, it is possible to rebuild those relationships and find joy in spending time with those who care about us most!

Remembering self-care isn't just about taking care of yourself physically; it's also about your mental well-being by connecting with people who make you feel safe and supported. Nurturing relationships with friends and family is a great way to practice self-care and ensure positive influences surround you.

Rebuilding Your Confidence and Sense of Self Worth

Narcissistic abuse is a form of emotional abuse that can have long-lasting psychological effects, including feelings of low self-worth and insecurity. It is essential to recognize the signs of narcissistic abuse so that you can take steps to protect yourself from further harm.

Recognizing the signs of narcissistic abuse is the first step in rebuilding your confidence and self-worth. This includes verbal, emotional, physical, or financial manipulation. It may also include gaslighting when someone makes you doubt your reality by denying facts or making false accusations. Additionally, narcissists often use guilt trips and intimidation tactics to control their victims.

Once you have identified the signs of narcissistic abuse, protect yourself from further harm. This includes setting boundaries with the abuser and seeking professional help if necessary. Practice self-care by engaging in activities that make you feel good about yourself, such as exercising, meditating, or spending time with friends and family who support you. Additionally, it can be helpful to talk about your experiences with others who have gone through similar situations, as this can help you feel less alone and more empowered.

Finally, remember that healing takes time and has ups and downs. It is common for survivors of narcissistic abuse to experience a range of emotions, such as anger, sadness, fear, guilt, shame, confusion, and even relief. It is important not to get discouraged during these times but instead focus on taking care of yourself emotionally and physically until you feel stronger again.

Rebuilding confidence and self-worth after narcissistic abuse takes time, but it is possible with patience and dedication. Recognizing the signs of narcissistic abuse early on and taking steps to protect yourself from further harm while engaging in activities that make you feel good about yourself will help you on your journey toward recovery.

Self-confidence is an essential part of living a fulfilling life. Here are some tips to help you boost your self-confidence and regain your self-worth:

1. Take care of yourself - Make sure you get enough sleep, eat healthy meals, and take time to relax and unwind. Taking care of your physical health will positively impact your mental well-being.

2. Surround yourself with positive people - Spend time with people who make you feel good about yourself and lift you up instead of bringing you down.

3. Set goals - Having something to work towards can give you a sense of purpose and accomplishment when you reach them.

4. Challenge yourself - Trying new things or pushing yourself out of your comfort zone can help build confidence in yourself and show that you're capable of more than what you thought possible.

5. Practice self-affirmations - Remind yourself daily that you are worthy and capable of achieving anything that comes your way.

Self-affirmations are a powerful tool for building self-confidence and belief in our abilities. By repeating positive statements about ourselves, we can help to counter negative thoughts and feelings that can lead to low self-esteem.

One of the most effective ways to use affirmations is to start with the words "I am" or "I will," followed by a present tense statement. This helps to create a sense of ownership over the affirmation, making it more likely to be accepted and internalized. It's also important to repeat your affirmations regularly; this helps them become part of your daily routine and makes them more likely to stick.

Another helpful technique is to list negative qualities you have identified in yourself, then write down an affirmation that counters each one. This can help you recognize and challenge unhelpful beliefs about yourself while reinforcing positive ones.

Finally, creating affirmation posters or cards is another great way to practice self-affirmation. You can put these up around your home or office as reminders of your positive statements throughout the day.

Setting meaningful goals is also essential to rebuilding your life after divorce and narcissistic abuse. Goals provide direction and motivation and help you stay focused on what you want to accomplish. To set meaningful goals, consider what you want to achieve, create a plan for how to get there, and take actionable steps toward reaching your goals.

When setting goals, make sure they are specific, measurable, achievable, relevant, and time-bound (SMART). This will help ensure that your goals are realistic and attainable. Additionally, break down your goal into smaller tasks to make it manageable. Finally, remember to reward yourself when you reach milestones!

With these tips, you can build up self-confidence and regain your self-worth.

Reconnecting With Your Self

One of the most vital steps in this journey is reconnecting with your self through introspection. This can help you find inner peace, gain clarity, and heal from the trauma of the experience.

Taking time for introspection after narcissistic abuse is essential in the healing process. It allows survivors to gain clarity on what happened and why and to understand their role in the situation. Through introspection, survivors can identify patterns of behavior that may have contributed to the abuse and start making changes that will help them heal and move forward. For example, people raised by a narcissistic parent may find themselves particularly vulnerable to entering into a narcissistic relationship. This is because they may have grown up in an environment where their needs were not met and their feelings were not validated, leading them to seek relationships replicating this dynamic.

Introspection also helps survivors gain insight into their feelings and emotions. This can be especially helpful for those conditioned by their abuser to suppress or ignore their needs and feelings. By taking time for self-reflection, survivors can start to recognize their emotional responses and learn how to manage them in the future better.

Finally, introspection after narcissistic abuse is essential for rebuilding trust in oneself and others. After experiencing such a traumatic event, it's natural for survivors to feel wary of forming new relationships or trusting other people again. Taking time for self-reflection can help survivors understand why they were vulnerable to narcissistic abuse in the first place and develop healthier boundaries when it comes to interacting with others moving forward.

In short, taking time for introspection after narcissistic abuse is essential for recovery and healing from this traumatic experience. It allows survivors to gain clarity on what happened, understand their role in the situation, recognize their emotions, and rebuild trust in themselves and others.

Joining Support Groups

Support groups can be invaluable resources for survivors of narcissistic abuse. They provide a safe space to share experiences, learn from others, and find support and validation. In these groups, survivors can talk openly about their experiences without fear of judgment or criticism. They can also gain insight into the dynamics of narcissistic abuse and understand how to cope with the aftermath of such trauma. Support groups provide a sense of community and belonging, essential for healing after narcissistic abuse. Through these groups, survivors can build resilience and develop skills to help them progress with greater self-confidence and self-worth.

Dating After Narcissistic Abuse

Dating after a narcissistic relationship can be overwhelming at first. Take the time to heal before beginning to date again. Several steps can help you on your journey, such as prioritizing your recovery, having no contact with the narcissist, educating yourself about Narcissistic Personality Disorder, accepting that you were victimized, and accepting that it will take time to trust someone again.

Here are some signs that you may be ready for dating after a narcissistic relationship:

1. You have taken the time to process your emotions and understand what happened in your previous relationship.

2. You have worked on building trust in yourself and others again.

3. You no longer project your past experiences onto potential partners.

4. You are aware of any anger or resentment that may come up and know how to manage it healthily.

5. You have done healing work to release the trauma from the past relationship and have made strides to alleviate it.

6. You can recognize red flags in prospective dates and move forward cautiously.

7. You can set boundaries with potential partners and communicate with them effectively.

8. You have spent enough time alone out of a relationship before meeting someone new so that you can make an informed decision about whether or not they are suitable for you.

When you feel ready to start dating again, become aware of red flags in prospective dates and move forward cautiously. Dating a narcissist can change someone in many ways, such as developing a deep distrust for men or feeling emotionally drained. Remember that recovery has no timetable, and pressure to date after narcissistic abuse can add to the emotional turmoil you feel after the relationship.

Here are some of the most common warning signs to look out for:

1. They make you feel bad about yourself.

2. They have you second-guessing their feelings toward you.

3. They don't listen to you.

4. They rush a new relationship forward too quickly.

5. They describe all of their exes as "crazy."

6. They're rude to people in the service industry or others they interact with in public settings.

7. Love bombing – when someone showers you with affection and gifts early on in a relationship before revealing their true colors later on down the line.

8. Moving too quickly – if your partner is pushing for commitment without getting to know each other first, this could be a sign that something isn't quite right.

9.

Not introducing you to their friends or family – if your partner keeps avoiding introducing you to the people closest to them, this could be a sign that they're not taking the relationship seriously enough or that they're hiding something from you about their past relationships or current situation at home/work/etc...

10. They never apologize or never apologize unless prompted to do so by someone else – this could indicate an unwillingness or inability to take responsibility for one's actions and accept blame when necessary, which can lead to further issues down the line in a relationship if left unchecked and unresolved over time.

11. Seeing your partner through rose-colored glasses – if you ignore obvious red flags because of how much you like them, it might be time for a reality check and reconsideration of whether this is the right person for you long-term.

12. Ignoring your gut feeling - If something doesn't feel right about your partner, trust your instincts and investigate further before investing more time and energy into the relationship.

In addition to looking out for red flags, it's also essential to look out for green flags. Green flags are signs that indicate a healthy and happy relationship. They can be subtle yet crucial indicators of compatibility between two people.

One of the most important green flags is respect for each other's boundaries. If your partner respects your boundaries and knows how to express their feelings, this is a great sign that you have a strong connection. It's also a good sign if they're stable and consistent in how they treat you.

Another key green flag is having good relationships with family and friends. This shows that they have strong interpersonal skills and can handle relationships well. Additionally, if they're open about their past and present life, they're comfortable with being vulnerable with you.

Finally, look out for signs of mutual respect in the relationship. If both partners show kindness towards each other, take responsibility for their actions, and make an effort to understand each other's point of view, this is an excellent indication that your relationship has the potential to be long-lasting and successful.

When looking for a partner or starting a new relationship, keep an eye out for these green flags, as they can indicate a healthy partnership in the future.

Lastly, taking the time necessary for healing is okay before entering into another relationship. This will help ensure you don't repeat patterns from your past relationships or become too vulnerable too quickly with someone new who may not be right for you yet. You can find love again after a narcissistic relationship with patience, understanding, and self-care!

Recovery from narcissistic abuse can be long and challenging, and there is no one-size-fits-all timetable for it. Everyone's experience is different, and the time it takes to heal can vary greatly depending on the nature and duration of the relationship and the depth of the abuse. It is important to remember that healing takes time and that you should not rush yourself or put pressure on yourself to move through the stages of recovery faster than you are comfortable with.

Understand that recovery involves more than just dealing with your emotions - it also requires finding skills, outlets, support, and self-care strategies that help you begin to heal. This may involve seeking professional help such as therapy or support groups. Taking care of your physical health by exercising, getting enough sleep, and eating nutritious food can also be beneficial in helping you recover from narcissistic abuse.

Several steps can be taken to help with recovery, such as acknowledging the loss, understanding that pain is normal, using your pain as motivation, talking about your feelings with friends and family, taking care of yourself, accepting how you feel, embracing coping skills, setting goals for yourself, and trying new hobbies. It is also important to remember that healing takes time, and everyone's healing process will look different.

It would help if you also let go of the need to understand why the abuser acted in specific ways and focus on your healing journey. As you progress through the stages of recovery, you will begin to blame yourself less and more fully heal from the trauma of narcissistic abuse.

No matter how long it takes, know you are not alone in this journey. Many resources are available to help you on your path toward healing and recovery after narcissistic abuse.

Chapter 12

Conclussion

N arcissistic abuse is a painful experience that can leave lasting emotional scars on a person's life. The road to healing from narcissistic abuse can be long and challenging, but it is possible. Empowering yourself to heal from narcissistic abuse is crucial to reclaiming your life and finding peace within yourself.

As a licensed clinical social worker, therapist, and coach, I understand the difficulties of navigating through the aftermath of narcissistic abuse. Acknowledging and validating the pain and trauma experienced by survivors is essential. Empathy and understanding are vital in this journey of healing.

One of the first steps towards healing from narcissistic abuse is recognizing and accepting that the abuse happened. Many survivors of narcissistic abuse struggle with denial or self-blame, which can prevent them from moving forward. It is important to understand that narcissistic abuse is not your fault, and you are not alone.

The healing process may involve therapy, support groups, and self-care practices focusing on self-love and self-compassion. These practices can help survivors regain control over their lives, heal from traumas, and rebuild their self-esteem.

Additionally, it is crucial to establish healthy boundaries and enforce them. This involves saying "no" to anything that makes you uncomfortable and prioritizing your needs over others. Setting healthy boundaries can be challenging, especially if you have a history of codependency or people-pleasing behaviors. But remember that establishing boundaries is necessary for your well-being.

In conclusion, healing from narcissistic abuse requires courage, self-awareness, and patience. Empowering yourself to heal is a process that takes time and effort, but it is worth it. By acknowledging the pain and trauma, seeking professional help, and practicing self-care and self-love, you can break free from the cycle of abuse and live a fulfilling life. Remember that you are not alone; with empathy and understanding, you can heal and reclaim your power.

Join Our Community

Are you currently struggling with a narcissistic relationship or recovering from narcissistic abuse? If so, I want to extend an invitation to you to join our online community.

Our community is a safe space where you can connect with others who have been through similar experiences and find support, resources, and guidance. Our members come from all over the world and have different backgrounds, but we share a common goal: to heal from narcissistic abuse and move forward in our lives.

Here, you can share your story, ask questions, and receive support and validation from others who understand what you're going through. Our community is moderated by experts in the field of narcissistic abuse and trauma recovery, so you can trust that you're in good hands.

Joining our private Facebook community is easy and free.

https://www.facebook.com/groups/unmaskingnarcissism

Don't suffer in silence any longer. You deserve to heal, and we're here to help. Join our community today and take the first step towards reclaiming your power and living the life you deserve.

Unmasking Narcissism Community With Kristin Fuller

http://www.unmaskingnarcissism.net

https://www.facebook.com/groups/unmaskingnarcissism

YouTube @UnMaskingNarcissism

Live To Thrive with Kristin Fuller MSW LCSW

www.livetothrive.net

YouTube @livetothrivecoach

About Kristin Fuller, LCSW

Kristin Fuller LCSW is an experienced licensed therapist and a graduate of The University of Georgia School of Social Work with a Master's Degree in Clinical Social Work, she has over 19 years of clinical experience and specializes in helping people escape and recover from narcissistic relationships. Kristin also helps those who have suffered trauma, depression, and anxiety to recover and rebuild their lives in her private practice.

Kristin has also been active in her community previously holding leadership positions as a committee chair with the National Association of Social Workers Georgia Chapter, creating volunteer programs and training for non-profit organizations such as Big Brother's Big Sisters Association and The Foster Children's Association, and contributing to fundraising projects with her children for organizations like the Salvation Army and Stand Up for Kids Atlanta. She also previously served as a board member with the Foster Children's Association lending her expertise with foster children and children's mental health.

Kristin resides northeast of Atlanta GA with her 2 children and enjoys reading, hiking, and spending time outdoors. Kristin has both personal and professional experience dealing with narcissism, which gives her a unique perspective on the topic - one that she is passionate about educating others about.

S ources

https://www.verywellmind.com/narcissistic-abuse-cycle-stages-impact-and-coping-6363187

https://www.verywellmind.com/narcissistic-abuse-cycle-stages-impact-and-coping-6363187

https://overcomewithus.com/narcissist-personality/the-narcissistic-abuse-cycle

https://www.choosingtherapy.com/narcissistic-abuse-cycle/

https://michaelgquirke.com/the-narcissistic-abuse-cycle-idealization-devaluation-rejection/

https://www.kaminiwood.com/the-narcissistic-abuse-cycle/

https://www.verywellmind.com/narcissistic-abuse-cycle-stages-impact-and-coping-6363187

https://michaelgquirke.com/the-narcissistic-abuse-cycle-idealization-devaluation-rejection/

https://www.kaminiwood.com/the-narcissistic-abuse-cycle/

https://overcomewithus.com/narcissist-personality/the-narcissistic-abuse-cycle

https://www.choosingtherapy.com/narcissistic-abuse-cycle/

https://www.choosingtherapy.com/narcissistic-abuse/

https://www.healthline.com/health/narcissistic-victim-syndrome

https://www.mindbodygreen.com/articles/narcissistic-abuse-15-signs-and-warnings-to-look-out-for

https://www.kaminiwood.com/9-signs-of-narcissist-hoovering-how-to-respond/

https://www.choosingtherapy.com/hoovering/

https://www.medicinenet.com/what_does_being_hoovered_mean/article.htm

https://www.insider.com/how-to-leave-a-narcissist-in-14-steps-2018-10

https://www.betterhelp

https://988lifeline.org/wp-content/uploads/2017/09/Brown_StanleySafetyPlanTemplate1.pdf

https://zerosuicide.edc.org/resources/resource-database/patient-safety-plan-template

https://www.therapistaid.com/therapy-worksheet/safety-plan

https://www.thehotline

https://www.choosingtherapy.com/narcissistic-manipulation-tactics/

https://abusewarrior.com/abuse/manipulation-tactics/

https://thriveworks.com/blog/how-narcissists-control-you/

https://www.forbes.com/health/mind/what-is-gaslighting/

https://www.verywellmind.com/is-someone-gaslighting-you-4147470

https://www.newportinstitute.com/resources/mental-
health/what_is_gaslighting_abuse/

https://en.wikipedia.org/wiki/Gaslighting

https://www.thehotline.org/resources/what-is-gaslighting/

https://www.mindbodygreen.com/articles/how-to-deal-with-gaslighting

https://positivepsychology.com/gaslighting-emotional-abuse/

https://www.psychologytoday.com/us/blog/mind-games/201904/

https://www.nytimes.com/2022/01/10/style/love-bombing.html

https://www.cosmopolitan.com/sex-love/a26988344/love-bombing-signs-
definition/

https://en.wikipedia.org/wiki/Love_bombing

https://www.bannerhealth.com/healthcareblog/teach-me/

https://happiful.com/what-is-love-bombing

https://www.kaminiwood.com/narcissist-triangulation-ending-the-manipulation/

https://www.choosingtherapy.com/narcissistic-triangulation/

https://www.healthline.com/health/narcissistic-triangulation

https://www.verywellmind.com/what-is-triangulation-in-psychology-5120617

https://www.marriage.com/advice/relationship/triangulation-in-relationships/

https://www.forbes.com/sites/traversmark/2022/10/31/

https://www.bates-communications.com/bates-blog/

https://www.healthline.com/health/narcissistic-triangulation

https://sugercoatit.com/direct-conversation-confident/

https://www.inc.com/anna-johansson/7-ways-to-start-a-conversation-that-leads-where-you-want-it-to.html

https://hbr.org/2017/05/how-to-have-difficult

https://www.choosingtherapy.com/narcissistic-manipulation-tactics/

https://www.psychologytoday.com/us/blog/narcissism-demystified/202109/8

https://thriveworks.com/blog/how-narcissists-control-you/

https://psychcentral.com/blog/psychology-self/2017/09/narcissistic-projection

https://thenarcissisticlife.com/narcissistic-projection/

https://www.carlacorelli.com/narcissistic-abuse-recovery/narcissistic-projection/

https://www.psychologytoday.com/us/basics/projection

https://www.healthline.com/health/projection-psychology

https://www.verywellmind.com/what-is-a-projection-defense-mechanism-5194898

https://www.psychologytoday.com/us/blog/narcissism-demystified/202006/7-ways-set-boundaries-narcissists

https://www.marriage.com/advice/counseling/dealing-with-narcissists-setting-boundaries/

https://psychcentral

https://www.helpguide.org/articles/mental-disorders/narcissistic-personality-disorder.htm

https://www.appliedbehavioranalysisprograms.com/lists/five-signs-narcissism/

https://www.webmd.com/mental-health/narcissism-symptoms-signs

https://www.psychologytoday.com/us/blog/invisible-bruises/202201/5-steps-surviving-narcissists-smear-campaign

https://narcissistabusesupport.com/red-flags/narcissistic-smears-narcissist-abuse-smear-campaigns/

https://abusewarrior.com/abuse/smear-campaign/

https://psychcentral.com/pro/exhausted-woman/2019/07/narcissists-and-their-flying-monkeys

https://www.psychologytoday.com/us/blog/women-autism-spectrum-disorder/202010/

https://unfilteredd.net/usage-of-flying-monkeys/

https://www.choosingtherapy.com/narcissistic-manipulation-tactics/

https://www.psychologytoday.com/us/blog/narcissism-demystified/202109/

https://overcomewithus.com/narcissist-personality/how-do-narcissists-manipulate

https://www.psychologytoday.com/us/blog/toxic-relationships/202102/tactics-narcissists-use-gain-power

https://psychologicalhealingcenter.com/narcissism-power-and-control/

https://pursuit.unimelb.edu.au/articles/it-s-official-power-creates-a-narcissist

https://www.goodtherapy.org/blog/overcoming-narcissistic-abuse-0813184

https://www.propsychologicalservicesllc.com/how-do-narcissists-use-manipulation/

https://psychcentral.com/disorders/narcissistic-personality-disorder/narcissistic-collapse

https://www.quora.com/Why-do-narcissists-need-to-degrade-you

https://www.verywellmind.com/narcissistic-abuse-cycle-stages-impact-and-coping

https://www.thehotline.org/

https://www.verywellmind.com/how-to-deal-with-verbal-abuse-5205616

https://psychcentral.com/health/how-to-deal-with-verbal-abuse

https://www.talkspace.com/mental-health/conditions/articles/how-to-set-boundaries-with-a-narcissist/

https://www.psychologytoday.com/us/blog/narcissism-demystified/202006/7-ways-set-boundaries-narcissists

https://www.caminorecovery.com/blog/why-its-important-to-set-boundaries-with

https://www.psychologytoday.com/us/blog/communication-success/202007/8-signs-of-a-narcissistic-communicator

https://www.grwhealth

https://www.merriam-webster.com/dictionary/compliment

https://dictionary.cambridge.org/us/dictionary/english/compliment

https://www.grammarly.com/blog/complement-compliment/

https://www.betterup.com/blog/grey-rocking

https://psychcentral.com/health/grey-rock-method

https://www.psychologytoday.com/us/blog/the-time-cure/202211/

https://www.healthline.com/health/grey-rock

https://www.medicalnewstoday.com/articles/grey-rock

https://psychologia.co/narcissist-no-contact/

https://www.bonobology.com/no-contact-narcissist/

https://toxicties.com/no-contact-narcissist-mistakes/

https://www.bonobology.com/no-contact-narcissist/

https://hetexted

https://www.youtube.com/watch?v=hN-RsF17_Mk

https://www.mindful.org/mindfulness-meditation-anxiety/

https://www.headspace.com/meditation/anxiety

https://primedmind.com/benefits-of-guided-meditation/

https://www.thehealthy.com/alternative-medicine/guided-meditation/

https://theculturetrip.com/europe/united-kingdom/articles/the-benefits-of-guided-meditation/

https://queenbeeing.com/8-powerful-self-care-tips-for-narcissistic-abuse-survivors/

https://www.centrepointpsychotherapy.com/self-care-while-loving-a-narcissist/

https://unmaskingthenarc.com/self-care-after-narcissistic

https://narcwise.com/2018/02/03/how-journaling-combats-gaslighting-to-free-you-from-narcissistic-abuse/

https://www.youtube.com/watch?v=xLiYzUljTNE

https://ineffableliving.com/journal-prompts-for-narcissistic-abuse/

https://www.incadence.org/post/music-therapy-as-treatment-for

https://digitalcommons.usu.edu/cgi/viewcontent.cgi?article=1121&context=honors

https://victimservicecenter.org/music-therapy-and-healing-trauma/

https://my.clevelandclinic.org/health/treatments/8817-music-therapy

https://petersonfamilyfoundation.org/news/health-benefits-of-music-therapy/

https://positivepsychology.com/music-therapy-benefits/

https://wisdomwithinct.com/narcissistic-abuse-trauma-counseling-cptsd-therapist/

https://advancedcounseling.info/counseling-narcissistic-abuse/

https://queenbeeing.com/find-therapist-understands-narcissistic-abuse-recovery-npd-10-powerful-questions/

https://www.psychologytoday.com/us/blog/chronically-me/201806/art-self-care

https://aquarryl.studio/art-as-self-care/

https://psychcentral.com/blog/9-ways-to-use-art-to-practice-self-care

https://www.lifed.com/7-ways-to-incorporate-more-art-into-your-daily-life/

https://keetonsonline.wordpress.com/2015/06/01/10-ways-to-get-more-art-into-your-life/

https://theroanokestar.com/2022/03/09/11-ways-to-integrate

https://www.tendacademy.ca/using-music-self-care/

https://musicworxinc.com/2022/03/29/music-creative-arts-for-self-care/

https://annamaria.edu/wp-content/uploads/2020/09/Katie-Parker-Fall-2019.pdf

https://www.creativesoulmusic.com/blog/11-ways-to-include-music-in-your-daily-life

https://www.incadence.org/post/

https://www.youtube.com/watch?v=yttwWhuX18A

https://www.mindful.org/a-guide-to-practicing-self-care-with-mindfulness/

https://www.psycom.net/10-minutes-that-can-change-your-life

https://www.youtube.com/watch?v=Tb-8YjLF9c0

https://www.youtube.com/watch?v=vlLwR2x9ekY

https://www.mindbodygreen.com/articles/how-to-balance-sacral-chakra

https://www.health.harvard.edu/exercise-and-fitness/the-4-most-important-types-of-exercise

https://www.nhsinform.scot/healthy-living/keeping-active/getting-started/types-of-exercise

https://www.medicinenet.com/four_most_important_types_of_exercises/article.htm

https://www.harpersbazaar.com/uk/beauty/fitness-wellbeing/a25626354/yoga-vs-pilates/

https://www.healthline.com/health/fitness-exercise/pilates-vs-yoga

https://www.webmd.com/fitness-exercise/difference-between-pilates-and-yoga

https://yourchoicenutrition.com/5-ways-to-practice-self-care-through-nutrition/

https://www.therealgoodnutrition.com/therealgoodblog/2019/3/25/good-nutrition-is-good-self-care

https://www.forbes.com/sites/nomanazish/2017/12/11/10-smart-ways-to

https://www.healthline.com/nutrition/29-healthy-snacks-for-weight-loss

https://www.delish.com/cooking/nutrition/g600/healthy-snacks-for-work/

https://snacknation.com/blog/guide/healthy-snacks/

https://www.health.harvard.edu/staying-healthy/how-much-water-should-you-drink

https://www.who.int/news-room/fact-sheets/detail/drinking-water

https://www.healthline.com/nutrition/7-health-benefits-of-water

https://www.healthline.com/nutrition/how-to-drink-more-water

https://www.everydayhealth.com/dehydration/hydration-hacks-that-help-you-drink-more-water/

https://www.cdc

https://www.healthline.com/nutrition/29-healthy-snacks-for-weight-loss

https://www.delish

https://www.herhappyheart.com/self-care-hobbies/

https://www.caring-crate.com/blogs/caring-crate-blog/hobbies-to-add-to-your-self-care-routine

https://www.bustle.com/p/15-old-fashioned-self-care-activities

https://www.linkedin.com/pulse/

https://theeverygirl.com/hobbies

https://www.mymentalhealth.guide/self-care/hobbies-relaxation

https://www.psychalive.org/narcissistic-relationships/

https://www.choosingtherapy.com/narcissistic-relationship/

https://www.healthline.com/health/mental-health/am-i-dating-a-narcissist

https://www.verywellmind.com/stages-of-healing-after-narcissistic-abuse-5207997

https://www.choosingtherapy.com/recovering-from-narcissistic-abuse/

https://tinybuddha.com/blog/healing-from-the-trauma-of-narcissistic-abuse/

https://overcomewithus.com/narcissist-personality/how-to-spot-an-overt-narcissist

https://www.linkedin.com/pulse/overt-narcissist-personality-disorder-adapted-from-article-collins

https://psychologicalhealingcenter.com/overt-narcissism/

https://www.verywellmind.com/understanding-the-covert-narcissist-4584587

https://health.clevelandclinic.org/covert-narcissism/

https://www.verywellhealth.com/covert-narcissistic-personality-disorder-5212505

https://en.wikipedia.org/wiki/Narcissism

https://www.webmd.com/mental-health/narcissism-symptoms-signs

https://www.helpguide.org/articles/mental-disorders/narcissistic-personality-disorder.htm

https://estd.org/narcissism-consequence-trauma-and-early-experiences

https://www.psychologytoday.com/us/blog/warning-signs-parents/201701/

https://www.pnas.org/doi/10.1073/pnas.1420870112

https://www.ncbi.nlm.nih.gov/pmc/articles/PMC7432641/

https://news.osu.edu/how-parents-may-help-create-their-own-little-narcissists/

https://www.pnas.org/doi/10.1073/pnas.1420870112

https://www.pnas.org/doi/10.1073/pnas.1420870112

https://www.nyu.edu/about/news-publications/news/2021/march/

https://www.psychologytoday.com/us/blog/finding-new-home/202202/what-new-research-is-telling-us

https://www.childwelfare.gov/pubpdfs/long_term_consequences.pdf

https://www.americanbar.org/groups/public_interest/child_law/resources/

https://developingchild.harvard.edu/science/deep-dives/neglect/

https://www.ncbi.nlm.nih.gov/pmc/articles/PMC7432641/

https://news.osu.edu/how-parents-may-help-create-their-own-little-narcissists/

https://www.pnas.org/doi/10.1073/pnas.1420870112

https://www.childwelfare.gov/pubpdfs/long_term_consequences.pdf

https://www.americanbar.org/groups/p

https://developingchild.harvard.edu/science/deep-dives/neglect/

https://www.npd.com/

https://en.wikipedia.org/wiki/Narcissistic_personality_disorder

https://www.psychologytoday.com/us/conditions/narcissistic-personality-disorder

https://www.helpguide.org/articles/mental-disorders/narcissistic-personality-disorder.htm

https://en.wikipedia.org/wiki/Narcissistic_personality_disorder

https://psychcentral.com/disorders/narcissistic-personality-disorder

https://www.ncbi.nlm.nih.gov/books/NBK556001/

https://www.theravive.com/therapedia/narcissistic-personality-disorder-dsm--5-301.81-(f60.81)

https://www.psychdb

https://aps.onlinelibrary.wiley.com/doi/10.1111/cp.12214

https://www.ncbi.nlm.nih.gov/pmc/articles/PMC5819598/

https://www.helpguide.org/articles/mental-disorders/narcissistic-personality-disorder.htm

https://en.wikipedia.org/wiki/Narcissistic_personality_disorder

https://my.clevelandclinic.org/health/diseases/9742-narcissistic-personality-disorder

https://www.self.com/story/love-bombing-signs

https://medium.com/relationship-stories/10-signs-youre-being-devalued-by-a-narcissist-d3f38e0f3f2a

https://www.quora.com/What-are-signs-that-you-are-being

https://medium.com/relationship-stories/10-signs-youre-being-discarded-by-a-narcissist-d292a6a8dad4

https://www.choosingtherapy.com/narcissist-discard/

https://www.quora.com/What-are-the-signs-of-being-discarded-by-a-narcissist

https://www.choosingtherapy.com/hoovering/

https://www.helpguide.org/articles/mental-disorders/narcissistic-personality-disorder.htm

https://en.wikipedia.org/wiki/Narcissistic_personality_disorder

https://my.clevelandclinic.org/health/diseases/9742-narcissistic-personality-disorder

https://www.psychotherapynetworker.org/article/challenging-narcissist

https://www.helpguide.org/articles/mental-disorders/narcissistic-personality-disorder.htm

https://www.psychologytoday.com/us/blog/in-it-together/201708/narcissism-and-capacity-change

https://www.mayoclinic.org/diseases-conditions/narcissistic-personality-disorder/

https://my.clevelandclinic.org/health/diseases/9742-narcissistic-personality-disorder

https://www.webmd.com/mental-health/narcissistic-personality-disorder

https://narcissistabusesupport.com/7-signs-the-narc-is-serving-you-a-word-salad/

https://narcwise.com/2018/05/22/narcissist-word-salad/

https://fairytaleshadows.com/word-salad-when-talking-is-a-narcissists-weapon/

https://narcissistabusesupport.com/7-signs-the-narc-is-serving-you-a-word-salad/

https://abusewarrior.com/abuse/narcissistic-word-salad/

https://queenbeeing.com/5-warning-signs-that-a-narcissist-is

https://queenbeeing.com/5-warning-signs-that-a-narcissist-is-serving-you-word-salad/

https://www.thoughtco.com/word-salad-definition-1692505

https://narcwise.com/2018/05/22/narcissist-word-salad/

https://www.psychologytoday.com/us/blog/the-narcissist-in-your-life/202107/

https://www.carlacorelli.com/narcissistic-abuse-recovery/the-five-types-of-narcissist-which-one-are-you

https://www.collinsdictionary.com/us/dictionary/english/antagonistic-relationship

https://psycnet.apa.org/record/2018-36041-018

https://www.fatherly.com/life/signs-you-are-too-antagonistic

https://www.universalclass.com/articles/writing/business-communication/conflict-resolution/

https://www.ncbi.nlm.nih.gov/pmc/articles/PMC1484830/

https://psycnet.apa.org/record/1969-15709-001

https://www.marriage.com/advice/mental-health/narcissist-mind-games/

https://psychcentral.com/blog/manipulation-games-narcissists-play

https://www.wengood.com/en/psychology/stress/art-narcissist-mind-games

https://www.thehotline.org/

https://en.wikipedia.org/wiki/Psychological_abuse

https://www.verywellmind.com/psychological-abuse-types-impact-and-coping-strategies-5323175

https://www.choosingtherapy.com/reactive-abuse/

https://triggeryourtrip.com/emotional-path/reactive-abuse/

https://thehotline.org/

https://www.thehotline.org/

https://www.choosingtherapy.com/reactive-abuse/

https://www.aconsciousrethink.com/18895/reactive-abuse/

http://www.leahsykestherapy.com/blog/2016/1/20/somatic-practices-to-reduce-anxiety

https://www.schoolofmodernpsychology.com/blog/2018/9/17/

https://psychcentral.com/lib/somatic-therapy-exercises

https://emdrfoundation.org/toolkit/butterfly-hug.pdf

https://www.counselingconnectionsnm.com/blog/try-the-butterfly-hug-to-help-with-ptsd-symptoms

https://www.today.com/health/mind-body/butterfly-hug-rainbow-breathing-relieve-stress-anxiety-rcna24055

https://www.bristolhypnotherapy.co.uk/blog/2018/06/paced-breathing-other-breathing.html

https://uhs.berkeley.edu/sites/default/files/breathing_exercises_0.pdf

https://www.health.harvard.edu/mind-and-mood/

https://manhattanpsychologygroup.com/dbt-tipp-skills/

https://dialecticalbehaviortherapy.com/distress-tolerance/tipp/

https://gatewelltherapycenter.com/2020/11/04/tip-skills-cope-distress/

https://www.urmc.rochester.edu/behavioral-health-partners/bhp-blog/april-2018/

https://insighttimer.com/blog/54321-grounding-technique/

https://www.choosingtherapy.com/54321-method/

https://www.verywellmind.com/visualization-for-relaxation-2584112

https://www.netcredit.com/blog/visualization-techniques-calm-anxious-mind/

https://www.therapistaid.com/worksheets/progressive-muscle-relaxation-script

https://www.law.berkeley.edu/files/Progressive_Muscle_Relaxation.pdf

https://www.baylor.edu/content/services/document.php/183466

https://www.healthline.com/health/breathing-exercises-for-anxiety

https://www.verywellmind.com/abdominal-breathing-2584115

https://www.forbes.com/health/mind/breathing-exercises-anxiety/

https://www.healthline.com/health/how-to-calm-down

https://www.everydayhealth.com/columns/therese-borchard-sanity-break/10-quick-ways-to-calm-down/

https://www.self.com/story/emotional-regulation-skills

https://www.healthline.com/health/mental-health/9-tips-for-narcissistic-abuse-recovery

https://www.verywellmind.com/effects-of-narcissistic-abuse-5208164

https://psychcentral.com/disorders/narcissistic-personality-disorder/narcissistic-abuse-recovery

https://www.talkspace.com/mental-health/conditions/articles/narcissistic-abuse/

https://medcircle.com/articles/narcissistic-abuse/

https://www.apa.org/ptsd-guideline/patients-and-families/cognitive-behavioral

https://www.mayoclinic.org/tests-procedures/cognitive-behavioral-therapy/about/pac-20384610

https://www.verywellmind.com/what-is-cognitive-behavior-therapy-2795747

https://www.psychologytoday.com/us/therapy-types/acceptance-and-commitment-therapy

https://en.wikipedia.org/wiki/Acceptance_and_Commitment_Therapy

https://contextualscience.org/act

https://www.verywellmind.com/dialectical-behavior-therapy-1067402

https://www.psychologytoday.com/us/therapy-types/dialectical-behavior-therapy

https://www.ncbi.nlm.nih.gov/pmc/articles/PMC2963469/

https://www.youtube.com/watch?v=W5mJGYKW4w8

https://insighttimer.com/lisaromano/guided-meditations/healing-from-narcissistic-abuse-and-rejection

https://queenbeeing.com/narcissistic-abuse-recovery-get-fog-mindfulness/

https://www.emdr.com/what-is-emdr/

https://centerfordiscovery.com/understanding-actually-happens-emdr-therapy/

https://www.webmd.com/mental-health/emdr-what-is-it

https://www.psychologytoday.com/us/therapy-types/somatic-therapy

https://www.verywellmind.com/what-is-somatic-therapy-5190064

https://psychcentral.com/blog/

https://arttherapy.org/

https://www.verywellmind.com/what-is-art-therapy-2795755

https://www.psychologytoday.com/us/therapists/tx/austin?category=art-therapy

https://www.mayoclinic.org/tests-procedures/massage-therapy/about/pac-20384595

https://health.clevelandclinic.org/benefits-of-massage/

https://www.nccih.nih.gov/health/massage-therapy-what-you-need-to-know

https://www.everydayhealth.com/narcissism/

https://www.goodtherapy.org/learn-about-therapy/issues/narcissism

https://goop.com/wellness/health/its-not-your-fault-youre-a-narcissist/

https://www.psychologytoday.com/us/therapy-types/transpersonal-therapy

https://www.goodtherapy.org/learn-about-therapy/types/transpersonal-psychotherapy

https://www.harleytherapy.co.uk/counselling/what-is-transpersonal-therapy.htm

https://ifs-institute.com/

https://en.wikipedia.org/wiki/Internal_Family_Systems_Model

https://www.goodtherapy.org/learn-about-therapy/types/internal-family-systems-therapy

https://www.hhs.texas.gov/providers/behavioral-health-services-providers

https://www.mayoclinic.org/diseases-conditions/mental-illness/in-depth/mental-health-providers/

https://www.talkspace.com/mental-health/conditions/articles/narcissistic-abuse/

https://www.verywellmind.com/effects-of-narcissistic-abuse-5208164

https://www.mindbodygreen.com/articles/narcissistic-abuse-15-signs-and-warnings-to

https://www.psychalive.org/narcissistic-relationships/

https://www.healthline.com/health/mental-health/am-i-dating-a-narcissist

https://www.choosingtherapy.com/narcissistic-relationship/

https://psychcentral.com/pro/exhausted-woman/2019/09/narcissistic-rescuers-beware-of-the-backlash

https://www.lovepanky.com/my-life/better-life/narcissistic-rage

https://www.goodtherapy.org/blog/blindsided-recovering-narcissistic-abuse-relationship-0607134

https://www.talkspace.com/mental-health/conditions/articles/narcissistic-abuse/

https://www.verywellmind.com/effects-of-narcissistic-abuse-5208164

https://www.mindbodygreen.com/articles/narcissistic-abuse-15-signs-and-warnings-to-look-out-for

https://www.survivedivorce.com/divorcing-narcissist

https://www.womansdivorce.com/divorcing-a-narcissist.html

https://www.berenjifamilylaw.com/divorcing-a-narcissist-tips-tools-and-what-to-expect/

https://www.talkspace.com/mental-health/conditions/articles/narcissistic-abuse/

https://www.verywellmind.com/effects-of-narcissistic-abuse-5208164

https://www.mindbodygreen.com/articles/narcissistic-abuse-15-signs-and-warnings-to-look-out-for

https://www.onemomsbattle.com/blog/divorcing-a-narcissist-finding-the-right-attorney

https://narcissistabusesupport.com/divorcing-a-narcissist-questions-to-ask-a-lawyer-before-you-hire-them/

https://memphisdivorce.com/divorce/divorcing-a-narcissist

https://www.onemomsbattle.com/blog/divorcing-a-narcissist-finding-the-right-attorney

https://memphisdivorce.com/divorce/divorcing-a-narcissist-six-family-lawyers-advice/

https://www.fathersrightsdallas.com/divorcing-a-narcissist/

https://memphisdivorce.com/divorce/stages-of-divorcing-a-narcissist-part-1/

https://www.survivedivorce.com/divorcing-narcissist

https://www.lynchowens.com/blog/2022/october/divorcing-a-narcissist-breaking-the-cycle-of-coe/

https://memphisdivorce.com/divorce/stages-of-divorcing-a-narcissist-part-1/

https://www.lynchowens.com/blog/2022/october/divorcing-a-narcissist-breaking-the-cycle-of-coe/

https://farzadlaw.com/divorcing-a-narcissist/how-does-a-narcissist-handle

https://memphisdivorce.com/divorce/stages-of-divorcing-a-narcissist-part-1/

https://www.lynchowens.com/blog/2022/october/divorcing-a-narcissist-breaking-the-cycle-of-coe/

https://www.womansdivorce.com/divorcing-a-narcissist.html

https://www.talkspace.com/mental-health/conditions/articles/narcissistic-abuse/

https://www.verywellmind.com/effects-of-narcissistic-abuse-5208164

https://overcomewithus.com/narcissist-personality/the-narcissistic-abuse-cycle

https://www.linkedin.com/pulse/narcissistic-abuse-family-court-systems-becausewemediated-

https://adzlaw.com/family-law/2021/06/11/how-to-deal-with-a-narcissist-in-court-proceedings/

https://psychcentral.com/pro/exhausted-woman/2016/03/how-narcissists-use-the

https://www.quora.com/How-do-narcissists-weaponize-the-court-system

https://www.mercurynews.com/2020/09/01/opinion-dealing-with-narcissists-in-the-family-law-courtroom

https://www.jdsupra.com/legalnews/how-to-identify-and-deal

https://www.wikihow.com/Destroy-a-Narcissist-in-Court

https://adzlaw.com/family-law/2021/06/11/how-to-deal-with-a-narcissist-in-court-proceedings/

https://www.quora.com/How-do-you-deal-with-a-narcissist-in

https://www.divorcenet.com/resources/top-tips-for-surviving-your-divorce-with-a-narcissist.html

https://www.lynchowens.com/blog/2022/october/divorcing-a-narcissist-breaking-the-cycle-of-coe/

https://farzadlaw.com/divorcing-a-narcissist/how-does-a-narcissist-handle-divorce-react-cope

https://www.macdowelllawgroup.com/library/what-to-expect-when

https://www.nytimes.com/guides/business/manage-a-successful-team

https://www.projectmanager.com/blog/assemble-a-project-team

https://hr.mit.edu/learning-topics/teams/articles/new-team

https://cornerstonelaw.us/setting-realistic-expectations-for-family-law/

https://farzadlaw.com/what-expect-family-law-judge

https://www.garynickelson.com/blog/2022/12/is-sole-custody-a-realistic-goal-in-your-texas

https://www.traviscountytx.gov/dro/family-court-services

https://en.wikipedia.org/wiki/Family_court

https://guides.sll.texas.gov/child-custody-and-support

https://www.verywellmind.com/what-is-narcissistic-rage-5183744

https://www.psychologytoday.com/us/blog/communication-success/201807/8-signs-of-narcissistic-rage

https://www.healthline.com/health/mental-health/narcissistic-rage

https://sbrownlawyer.com/2021/03/15/

https://www.claytoncountyga.gov/government/courts/magistrate-court/

https://www.law.cornell.edu/wex/guardian_ad_litem

https://www.ptla.org/what-guardian-ad-litem

https://www.andersondivorcelaw.com/orland-park-attorney/

https://www.galmichelawfirm.com/blog/2016/november/when-should-a-guardian

https://www.helpguide.org/articles/parenting-family/co-parenting-tips-for-divorced-parents.htm

https://www.verywellfamily.com/signs-of-a-healthy-coparenting-relationship-2997282

https://raisingchildren.net.au/grown-ups/family

https://en.wikipedia.org/wiki/Emotion

https://www.verywellmind.com/what-are-emotions-2795178

https://www.britannica.com/science/emotion

https://www.verywellfamily.com/signs-of-a-healthy-coparenting-relationship-2997282

https://www.fatherhood.gov/dadtalk-blog/what-does-healthy-co-parenting-look

https://www.helpguide.org/articles/parenting-family/com

https://www.divorcemag.com/articles/talking-to-your-children-about-their-other-parent

https://www.jbdalessandrolaw.com/positivity-about-your-co-parent/

https://www.ourfamilywizard.com/blog/10-positive-co-parenting-tips

https://family.lovetoknow.com/co-parenting-communication

https://parentinganddivorceclass.com/wp-content/uploads/2017/03/A

https://familipay.com/blog/co-parenting-with-a-toxic-ex/

https://www.verywellfamily.com/types-of-parenting-styles-1095045

https://parentingscience.com/parenting-styles/

https://www.verywellmind.com/parenting-styles-2795072

https://www.ourfamilywizard.com/blog/communication-parallel-parenting-arrangement

https://www.verywellfamily.com/what-is-a-parallel-parenting-plan-and-how-to-make-one-5208661

https://farzadlaw.com/california

https://www.psychologytoday.com/us/blog/communication-success/201602/10-signs-narcissistic-parent

https://www.choosingtherapy.com/narcissistic-parent/

https://www.newportinstitute.com/resources/mental-health/narcissistic-parent/

https://www.parents.com/parenting/best-co-parenting-apps/

https://www.wealthysinglemommy.com/best-co-parenting-apps/

https://apps.apple.com/us/app/talkingparents-co-parent-app/id1092220726

https://www.choosingtherapy.com/narcissistic-abuse-cycle/

https://michaelgquirke.com/the-narcissistic-abuse-cycle-idealization-devaluation-rejection/

https://www.verywellmind.com/narcissistic-abuse-cycle-stages-impact-and-coping-6363187

https://blog.melanietoniaevans.com/forgiving-yourself-for-being-hooked-and

https://www.healthline.com/health/stages-of-grief

https://www.verywellmind.com/five-stages-of-grief-4175361

https://en.wikipedia.org/wiki/Five_stages_of_grief

https://amfmtreatment.com/trauma-bonding-what-is-it-and-why-do-we-do-it/

https://broxtowewomensproject.org.uk/trauma-bonding/

https://psychcentral.com/blog/recovering-narcissist/2019/03/

https://www.healthline.com/health/mental-health/trauma-bonding

https://www.forbes.com/health/mind/what-is-trauma-bonding/

https://www.medicalnewstoday.com/articles/trauma-bonding

https://www.choosingtherapy.com/how-to-break-a-trauma-bond/

https://www.modernintimacy

https://www.verywellmind.com/how-to-boost-your-self-confidence-4163098

https://au.reachout.com/articles/how-to-build-self-confidence

https://zenhabits.net/25-killer-actions-to-boost-your-self

https://www.washingtonpost.com/wellness/2022/05/02/do-self-affirmations-work/

https://www.healthline.com/health/mental-health/do-affirmations-work

https://www.forbes.com/health/mind/positive-affirmations/

https://www.wikihow.com/Set-Goals

https://www.betterup.com/blog/how-to-set-goals-and-achieve-them

https://www.mindtools.com/a5ykiuq/personal-goal-setting

https://grace-being.com/love-relationships/narcissistic-abuse-and-spiritual-awakening/

https://www.danaarcuri.com/post/spiritual-awakening-after-narcissistic-abuse

https://blog.melanietoniaevans.com/the-spiritual-war-of-narcissistic-abuse/

https://www.marriage.com/advice/mental-health/stages

https://narcissisticabuserecovery.online/support-group/

https://www.instagram.com/narcabusesquad/?hl=id

https://rayofsolace.com/narcissistic-abuse-support-groups/

https://personalityunleashed.com/dating-after-narcissistic-abuse/

https://medium.com/the-virago/

https://esme.com/single-moms/dating/dating-after-a-narcissist

https://www.marriage.com/advice/mental-health/stages-of-healing-after-narcissistic-abuse/

https://www.choosingtherapy.com/stages-of-healing-after-narcissistic-abuse/

https://psychcentral.com/disorders/narcissistic-personality-disorder/narcissistic-abuse-recovery

https://medium.com/the-virago/

https://personalityunleashed.com/dating-after-narcissistic-abuse/

https://esme.com/single-moms/dating/dating-after-a

https://www.garbo.io/blog/early-dating-red-flags

https://www.mindbodygreen.com/articles/green-flags-in-relationships

https://www.theguardian.com/lifeandstyle/2023/jan/28/6

https://www.womenshealthmag.com/sex-and-love/a42244790/green-flags-in-relationships/

Printed in Great Britain
by Amazon

20374207R00120